THE FAMILY:
BIBLICAL AND PSYCHOLOGICAL
FOUNDATIONS

Kalman J. Kaplan, M.W. Schwartz
and
Moriah Markus-Kaplan

To our families:
past, present, future
with special acknowledgment
to the memory of Haim Saposnik (A.H.)

THE JOURNAL OF PSYCHOLOGY AND JUDAISM is dedicated to exploring the relationship between psychology and Judaism and examines this relationship on both a clinical and philosophical level. The *Journal* publishes articles that are related to the spheres of psychology and Judaism and have implications concerning the synthesis of the two areas. The *Journal* serves as a forum for discussion and development of integrated approaches to uniquely Jewish problems in the clinical and meta-clinical realms.

MANUSCRIPTS should be submitted in triplicate to the Editor, Dr. Reuven P. Bulka, *Journal of Psychology and Judaism*, 1747 Featherston Drive, Ottawa, Ontario, Canada, K1H 6P4. Manuscripts should be typed on one side of the page, double-spaced throughout, on 8½" x 11" paper. A margin of at least one inch should be left on all sides. A title page should contain the names of all authors and sufficient addresses. A biography of 50-75 words should be included, (academic degress, professional interests, publications), along with a full face photograph. An abstract of no more than 100 words should accompany the manuscript. References should be listed following they style used by the American Psychological Association Publication Manual, 2nd ed. (1974). Citations from the *Bible, Talmud, Midrash, Maimonides, Shulchan Arukh, etc.,* should be incorporated into the text in parentheses following the pertinent quote or statement. The reference should refer to the overall work, not the specific volume. Where possible, references should identify standard English translations of the aforementioned works. Further information concerning the preparation of manuscripts can be obtained from the Editor, Articles and books for review should be mailed to The Critical Review, 3808 Severn Road, Cleveland Heights, Ohio 44118.

SUBSCRIPTIONS are made on an academic year basis; $16.00 per year. Institutional rates are $36. Prices slightly higher outside the United States. ADVERTISING and subscription inquiries should be made to: Human Sciences Press, 72 Fifth Avenue, N.Y., N.Y. 10011, (212)243-6000.

INDEXED in: Psychological Abstracts, Index to Jewish Periodicals, Current Contents/Social and Behavioral Sciences, Religious and Theological Abstracts, Social Sciences Citation Index, Selected Lists of Tables of Contents of Psychiatric Periodicals Modern Language Association International Bibliography, Guide to Social Science and Religion in Periodical Literature, and Pastoral Care and Counseling Abstracts.

LC77-647452   ISSN 0070-9801   JPJUD8(2)73-204(1984)

JOURNAL OF
psychology
AND
judaism

Volume 8, Number 2, Spring/Summer 1984

Library of Congress Number 77-647-452
ISBN: 0-89885-214-5
Copyright 1984 by Human Sciences Press

HUMAN SCIENCES PRESS
72 Fifth Avenue
New York, New York 10011

Printed in the United States of America

About The Authors

DR. KALMAN J. KAPLAN is presently Visiting Professor in the Department of Psychiatry and the Behavioral Sciences at Northwestern University Medical School. He received his A.B. from Northwestern University and his A.M. and Ph.D. from the University of Illinois. His specialty training at Northwestern involved mathematics, literature and psychology. At Illinois, his specialty was social psychology. Dr. Kaplan took a position in 1967 at Wayne State University where he was chairman of the Social Psychology program from 1979-1982 and is now Professor of Psychology. Dr. Kaplan has held visiting appointments at the University of California (Davis), Bell Laboratories, the Hebrew University of Jerusalem, both the Departments of Psychology and Social Relations and the Divinity School at Harvard University and Haifa University. Dr. Kaplan is also a Certified Social Worker and a Licensed Psychologist and has worked with individuals, couples and families.

DR. M. W. SCHWARTZ holds a Ph.D. in Ancient History from Wayne State University . He has taught History and Judaics at several universities in the United States and Canada. His special interests are Judaism of the Second Commonwealth Period, the Bible and Graeco-Roman civilization. He has also done extensive graduate work in psychology, marriage therapy, and pastoral counselling.

DR. MORIAH MARKUS-KAPLAN is presently teaching in the School of Education at Tel Aviv University and doing private clinical work. She received her A.B. and M.A. from The Hebrew University of Jerusalem and her Ph.D. from Boston University. Her specialty areas at Hebrew University were statistics and clinical psychology. Her specialty at Boston University was social psychology. In addition, Dr. Markus-Kaplan has received clinical training at Brandeis University and at Forest Hospital in Des Plaines, Illinois. During that time, Dr. Markus-Kaplan has taught courses at Boston University, Boston College and Harvard University. She will be at the Olden Adult Program in the Institute of Psychiatry at Northwestern University Medical School beginning in September, 1984.

ACKNOWLEDGMENTS

The drawing on the front cover has been prepared by Andre Naghiadas and is meant to denote the contrasting stories of Narcissus and Jonah. The red axis depicts three episodes in Narcissus' life: (1) his rejecton of the nymph Echo (position C); (2) his falling in love with the face in the brook (position A); and (3) his recognition of the face as his own and his subsequent suicide (position AC). The blue axis denotes three episodes in Jonah's life: (1) the fish saving him from drowning after he runs away in confusion from God's command (position B); (2) the fish vomiting Jonah out onto dry land after he prayed to God from the belly of the fish (position E); and (3) Jonah subsequently following God's commandment to go to Nineveh (position D). The initial versions of Figures 4 and 7 were prepared by John Douglas Clyde. We would also like to thank Fran Calabro and Rose Jenkins for their time and patience in deciphering our often illegible handwriting. The enthusiastic support, encouragement, and editing of this project by Dr. Reuven Bulka have also been greatly appreciated.

ABSTRACT

This treatise is aimed at contrasting Greek (narcissistic) and Hebrew (covenantal) models of marriage and family. Traditional psychoanalytic models are based on Greek archetypes such as Narcissus, Laius and Oedipus, and Clytemnestra and Electra and thus may not fully describe the dynamics underlying the Jewish family. Biblical archetypes such as Jonah, Abraham and Isaac, and Naomi and Ruth are suggested in an attempt to explain the peculiarly successful integration of intimacy and autonomy themes traditionally prized in Jewish families, and a possible resolution of the conflict between the sexes and the generations so rampant in Greek (and Western) families.

Narcissus vacillates between detached individuation (position C) and deindividuated attachment (position A), finally arriving at a suicidal juxtaposition of the two states (he comes to idealize his mirror reflection). Jonah, in contrast, avoids these narcissistic alternatives, his covenant with God allowing him to withdraw temporarily to a protected position (B) of deindividuated detachment and to advance at his own pace to a position of individuated attachment (D). In the ambivalent resolution of the oedipal and Electra dilemmas available to the Greek family, the sons become C personalities (mirroring narcissists), and the daughters become A personalities (idealizing narcissists). This sets the stage for a rejection-intrusion marriage in the next generation, perpetuating the cycle. The covenantal resolution available to the Jewish family, symbolized by circumcision and the laws of purification of the menstruant, creates a safe space for both sons and daughters to remain as B personalities and ultimately advance to the D position. This sets the stage for a reciprocal marriage in the next generation and works to overcome cultural narcissism.

Editor's Perspective

This issue of the *Journal of Psychology and Judaism* is special in many ways.

It is considerably larger than a regular issue of the journal.

It constitutes a complete book rather than a collection of separate articles on various subjects.

But the main reason this is special is the importance of this topic. This is a unique example of historical cross-cultural comparison, fusing psychology and Judaism.

The authors—Kalman J. Kaplan, M.W. Schwartz, and Moriah Markus-Kaplan—have pooled their considerable talents into a work of excellence, examining on a multi-dimensional level the interplay between the ancient Greek and Hebrew cultures—the differences, the myths and the misunderstandings in the roots of modern thinking.

The focus is on marriage and the family, and on the differences between the narcissistic and the covenantal, between the Greek and the Hebrew. The authors weave an intriguing web around their theme, and their findings are illuminating, even instructive.

I ended the Editor's Perspective for Volume 7, Number 1, by welcoming Kalman J. Kaplan to the journal's editoral board, referring to him as "a seminal contributor in the past and already with a few more pieces slated for publication shortly in this journal."

The pieces have grown into a book in collaboration wth M.W. Schwartz and Moriah Markus-Kaplan, and the *Journal of Psychology and Judaism* is proud to present their work in its pages.

Reuven P. Bulka
Editor

Publisher's note: Spellings of Hebrew names and titles of works in religious literature throughout are based on *The New Standard Jewish Encyclopedia*, 5th ed., 1977.

Journal of Psychology and Judaism, Vol. 8(2), Spring/Summer 1984
© *1984 Human Sciences Press*

CHAPTER I

Introduction

One of the major dichotomies in Western thought is the contrast between Hebraism and Hellenism. Indeed, this is the subject and title of two famous "Chapter Fours" in modern intellectual history—in Matthew Arnold's *Culture and Anarchy* (1932) and William Barrett's *Irrational Man* (1962). Although obviously oriented in opposite directions (Arnold toward Hellenism and Barrett toward Hebraism), they agree that the world (at least the Western world) has veered between those two alternatives. For Arnold, Hellenism represents "sweetness and light" and Hebraism "sin," Hellenism "spontaneity of consciousness" and Hebraism "strictness of conscience." Barrett's view of Hebraism, although primarily limited to the Old Testament, is somewhat more sophisticated. Among his distinctions are the following: (1) Hebraism extols the man of faith; Hellenism, the man of reason; (2) Hebraism is concrete; Hellenism is abstract; (3) Hebraism stresses commitment; Hellenism, detachment.

The study of Greek life has been idealized. Gilbert Murray, for example, writes that "Greek thought, always sincere and daring, was seldom brutal, seldom ruthless or cruel." In his thought-provoking work on the Greek family, Philip Slater (1968) looks beneath this mask at the often quite violent reality. Further, he stresses that in many ways Western man is Greek man (and by extension, Western family is the Greek family). This certainly seems to square with Freud's usage of Greek myths, such as those of Narcissus, Oedipus, and Electra, as underpinnings for psychoanalysis, and with Dodds's work on *The Greeks and the Irrational.*

With several exceptions (notably David Bakan and Erich Wellisch), no comparable attempt has been made to apply a Hebraic analysis to a study of interpersonal and familial relationships. That is the subject of this work: an attempt to contrast Hellenic and Hebraic motifs in interpersonal and familial relationships and to suggest how a covenantal view of families overcomes cultural narcissism.

The questions of which sources of information can be used and of what can be learned from them are integral. Our primary sources are the literatures of classical antiquity and of the biblical and rabbinic tradition. These sources do not provide a total historical picture, and there are few statistics of any value. What the sources can tell us is

Journal of Psychology and Judaism, Vol. 8(2), Spring/Summer 1984
©*1984 Human Sciences Press*

that certain themes appear in the literature and apparently held some currency in their time. When a theme appears often, it is fair to assume that it was important to the society in which it appeared.

The Hebrew Bible is, of course, an open book considered sacred to hundreds of millions of non-Jews, as well as to Jews, and it is subject to a wide variety of interpretations. The Jews' own views and usages of the biblical stories and laws are explained in the rabbinic literature, which has developed over many centuries. In order to establish that a given interpretation of a biblical story can be considered Jewish, one must show that the interpretation is derived from or is at least consistent with the views of rabbinic commentators. Not all rabbinic material on the family is entirely monolithic. Rabbinic sages debated issues of family relationships as they did most other matters; however, the praise of family life stands forth significantly in the rabbinic writings, with nothing to contradict it. It is significant that Jewish sources, both biblical and rabbinic, are characteristically unsparing in telling the truth about their protagonists, for both praise and blame.

Our data on Greek family and society come largely from a variety of ancient writings. We have found the Athenian drama of the fifth century B.C.E. especially useful. These plays were written by brilliant men such as Aeschylus, Sophocles, and Euripides who provide a penetrating insight into their own world. In particular, many plays concentrate on the story of Agamemnon and his family or on Oedipus. This is not to argue that every Greek family had so sordid a history as these; however, these stories, most of which originate in early and widely known Greek myths, became part and parcel of the thought repertoire of the Greeks. They both reflected and provided them with role models very different from those represented in the biblical families of Abraham and his descendants. Furthermore, the pattern of the Greek family that the plays present is borne out in great measure in the writings of Plato, Plutarch, Theognis of Megara, and other well-known authors of antiquity. Finally, they provide foundation myths (Narcissus, Oedipus, and Electra) for psychoanalysis, reflecting a conflictual pattern that, we argue, is overcome in the covenantal Jewish family.

Another methodological point must be made. Many of the citations we employ are from the rabbinic literature. On the one hand, although the rabbis were not unaware of many of the social benefits that arose from the observance of the Torah, they saw these benefits as secondary to the fulfilling of the divine commandments as an act of love for God. On the other hand, anthropologists often stress social benefits as the justification for a particular ritual. For example, an anthropologist might stress circumcision as a rite of passage, as it was to several ancient peoples other then the Jews. Circumcision was practiced by the Jews as part of their covenant with God. There is no discussion in the Hebrew Bible of any of its other possible benefits. The rabbinic tradition would be uninterested in the types of interpretations anthropologists use to explain religious rituals. We shall deal here with both aspects.

We also should point out that many psychoanalytic terms employed in this work seem to have been used by Freud in both a literal and general sense. For example, "fear of castration" can be taken in both its specific content and its more symbolic overtones. A similar analysis can be made of "menstrual shame." This two-layered meaning structure also informs our discussion of biblical customs such as "covenantal circumcision" and "covenantal purification of the menstruant."

A certain developmental pattern will become obvious to the reader in the course of this volume. The earlier chapters (2–6) primarily summarize dominant views of Greek and Hebrew cultural motifs. The later chapters (7–11) focus on our interpretations of specific interpersonal and familial narratives (e.g., Narcissus and Jonah, Oedipus and Isaac, Electra and Ruth). As this work has proceeded, our separate trainings in psychology, history, and religions have melded together. However, in some instances we have not found it possible totally to reconcile disparate methods, representations, and conclusions. Moriah Markus-Kaplan concentrated on the writing of chapters 2, 3, 5 and 11; M. W. Schwartz on chapters 1, 4, 6, 7, 8, 9, 10, and 11; and Kalman J. Kaplan on chapters 1–11 inclusively.

CHAPTER 2

Covenant and Contract: The Problem of Possibility and Necessity

This chapter will present some of the established views on covenantal and contractual approaches to relationships and their workings in the human personality. In subsequent chapters we shall present our redefinition of these important concepts and the resulting implications for an understanding of narcissism in individual, marital, and familial life.

Covenant and Contract

A succinct expression of the opposition between covenant and contract emerges from the work on religious philosophy, *Athens and Jerusalem,* by Lev Shestov (1966). In this work Shestov, schooled in Western philosophy and grounded in the Hebrew Bible,[1] explores the conflict throughout Western civilization between the epistemologies of objective reason (Athens) and subjective revelation (Jerusalem). As a prototype of this division, Shestov offers the figures of Abraham and Socrates.

> When God says to Abraham, "Leave your country, your friends and your father's house, and go to the land that I will show you," Abraham obeys and "leaves without knowing where he is going." And it is said in scripture that Abraham believed God, who imputed it to him for righteousness. All this is according to the Bible. But common sense judges quite otherwise. He who goes without knowing where he is going is a weak and frivolous man, and a faith which is founded on nothing (now faith is always founded on nothing, for it is faith itself that wishes to "found") cannot be in any way "imputed for righteousness." The same conviction, clearly and neatly formulated and raised to the level of method, reigns in science, which was born of common sense. . . . The believer goes forward, without looking to the right or to the left, without asking where he is going, without calculating. The scientist will not take a step without looking around him, without asking, and is afraid to budge from his place and wishes to know beforehand where he will arrive. (Shestov, 396–397)

This, for Shestov, is the contrast between Abraham and Socrates.

Journal of Psychology and Judaism, Vol. 8(2), Spring/Summer 1984
© 1984 Human Sciences Press

One who emulates Socrates "looks before he leaps,"[2] whereas one who emulates Abraham "leaps before he looks." Shestov argues that this represents the distinction between contract and covenant. Abraham agrees to accept the covenant with God without preconditions other than mutual fidelity (the destination of his journey is not specified in advance), allowing the terms of the covenant to reveal themselves slowly to the two participants. Indeed, the Hebrew Bible can be seen from this perspective as the working out of the Abrahamic covenant.

This difference in orientation with respect to two primary child-sacrifice narratives in the Hebrew and Greek civilizations has been highlighted by Franz Rosenzweig in his study of Abraham's offering of his son Isaac to God (the *akedah)* and of Agamemnon's offer of his daughter Iphigenia to Artemis, the goddess of the hunt (see Rosenzweig's exchange of letters with Eugen Rosenstock-Huessy [1969] on Judaism and Christianity). For Agamemnon, Iphigenia is a possession; he offers to sacrifice what he has in return for good winds to sail his fleet to Troy. This is what we mean by a simple *quid pro quo* contract. For Abraham, Isaac is far more than a possession, it is his link to God's promise to make of his seed a great nation. He is offering to sacrifice the "child of the promise" to the "God of the promise." Thus, Abraham is offering to sacrifice what he is and can be without thought of reward. This is what we mean by the essence of covenant.

A third perspective on this same problem is that offered by Martin Buber in his distinction between I-Thou and I-it relationships (Buber, [1958] 1970). It is admittedly very difficult to do justice to this rich and poetic distinction in such a short space. For our purposes, however, it can be said that in an I-Thou relation the "thou" is known directly as an end; in an I-it relation the "it" is perceived indirectly as a means. In other words, to stretch the point somewhat, an I-Thou relationship is a covenant relationship, where trust in the other precedes evidence (Buber, 1961). In contrast, the I-it relationship may be said to be a contract relationship, knowledge of the other always following the careful weighing of evidence.

This points to the common thread underlying Buber's distinction between I-Thou and I-it, Rosenzweig's distinction between Abraham and Agamemnon, and finally, Shestov's distinction between Abraham and Socrates. All point to the same duality in epistemological bias. A covenant depends on a "leap of faith" and pushes toward an unqualified commitment. A contract depends on prior evidence and allows only a qualified commitment. In other words, a covenant proceeds *a priori*, whereas a contract proceeds *a posteriori*. However, as we shall attempt to show in later chapters (especially 3 and 7), such

a division does not do full justice to the intricate development of real-
life relations. This demands a redefinition of covenant.

Schizophrenia and Depression

A penetrating discussion of the opposition of schizophrenic and
depressive psychoses emerges in the synthesis of psychoanalysis and
religion, *The Denial of Death* by Ernest Becker (1973). Becker,
grounded in cultural anthropology as well as in psychoanalytic
thought, follows Kierkegaard ([1849]1954) in delineating possibility
and necessity as two opposing pulls on the person.

> Too much possibility is the attempt by the person to overvalue the
> powers of the symbolic self. It reflects the attempt to exaggerate one
> half of the human dualism at the expense of the other. In this sense,
> what we call schizophrenia is an attempt by the symbolic self to deny
> the limitations of the finite body; in doing so, the entire person is pulled
> off balance and destroyed. It is as though the freedom of creativity that
> stems from within the symbolic self cannot be contained by the body,
> and the person is torn apart. This is how we understand schizophrenia
> today, as the split of self and body, a split in which the self is unan-
> chored, unlimited, not bound enough to everyday things, not contained
> enough in dependable physical behavior. . . . If schizophrenic psychosis
> is on a continuum of a kind of normal inflation of inner fantasy, of sym-
> bolic possibility, then something similar should be true of depressive
> psychosis. Depressive psychosis is the extreme on the continuum of too
> much necessity, that is, too much finitude, too much limitation by the
> body and the behaviors of the person in the real world, and not enough
> freedom of the inner self, of inner symbolic possibility. This is how we
> understand depressive psychosis today: as a bogging down in the
> demands of others—family, job, the narrow horizon of daily duties. In
> such a bogging down the individual does not feel or see that he has alter-
> natives, cannot imagine any choices or alternate ways of life, cannot
> release himself from the network of obligations even though these
> obligations no longer give him a sense of self-esteem, of primary value,
> of being a heroic contributor to world life even by doing his daily family
> and job duties. (Becker, 1973, 76-78)

For Becker then, the schizophrenic is not adequately built into the
world; the depressive on the other hand is built into the world too over-
whelmingly. Kierkegaard ([1849] 1954) puts it this way: "But while
one sort of despair plunges wildly into the infinite and loses itself, a
second sort permits itself as it were to be defrauded by 'the others' "
(166–167).

For Otto Rank ([1932] 1968) the question is one of the narrowing down of life, of how big a chunk of life to "bite off." Rank calls this "partialization"; Becker calls it "fetishization"—but the problem is the same for each of them, as are the opposing syndromes of neuroses they postulate. For Rank some individuals partialize (or fetishize) too much, bite off too small a chunk of life; others have difficulty partializing (or fetishizing) enough, have too vivid an imagination, take in too much experience and generally "bite off more than they can chew." The first type, for Rank, merges with the world around and becomes too much a part of it, and so loses the claim to life. The second type, on the other hand, cuts the self off from the world in order to make one's own complete claim and so loses the ability to live and act in the world on its terms. As Rank put it, some individuals are unable to separate and others are unable to unite, the first having too great a "fear of life" and the second too great a "fear of death."

A third perspective on this problem is given by Karen Horney (1950) in her distinction between expansive and self-effacing solutions to neurosis emerging from the split between the "real" and "ideal" self. She views the first solution as an "appeal of mastery" and the second as an "appeal of love." A complete discussion of Horney's distinction obviously lies beyond the scope of the present chapter. For our purposes, however, it can be said that the expansive individual glorifies and cultivates in the self everything that means mastery, tends to manipulate or dominate others and to make them dependent. The self-effacing individual, in contrast, tends to subordinate the self to others, to be dependent on them, to appease them, and cultivates in the self everything that means helplessness and suffering. Such an individual longs for help, protection, and surrendering love that will save the self. In other words, the expansive individual may tend to concentrate too much on possibility, underpartializing and thus trying to swallow whole the chunks he encounters. The self-effacing individual, in contrast, may tend to concentrate too much on necessity, becoming paralyzed in comparison by the multiplicity of the chunks one tries to take in.

This points to the common thread underlying Horney's distinction between expansion and self-effacement, Rank's distinction between underpartialization and overpartialization, and Becker's distinction between schizophrenic and depressive psychosis. All point to the same duality in epistemological bias. Possibility depends on a "leap of faith" beyond the present and pushes toward open relationships. Necessity depends on prior evidence and allows only closed relationships. In other words possibility proceeds *a priori* while necessity proceeds *a posteriori*. However, as we shall attempt to show in Chapters 3 and 7, such a division does not do full justice to the intricate development of real-life relations, nor does it allow a sufficiently rich definition of schizophrenia.

Commitment and Psychosis

The previous two sections have attempted to develop the relationship between epistemological bias and commitment on the one hand and between epistemological bias and psychosis on the other. Let us now try to draw our own parallel between these two lines of development.

The point of departure for Shestov is the contrast between one who, emulating Abraham, "leaps before he looks," and one who, emulating Socrates, "looks before he leaps." This dichotomy is parallel to that offered by Becker between one who lives life pulled ahead too much by possibility and one who lives held back too much by necessity. Shestov's Abraham can be seen as one underconcerned with necessity, leaping forward blindly into possibility. Shestov's Socrates, on the other hand, can be seen as one underconcerned with possibility, looking backward, paralyzed into necessity. This dichotomy is accepted by both Shestov and Becker.

A comparison of Rosenzweig and Rank sharpens this parallel. For Rosenzweig the essence of Abraham is to leap ahead of the evidence, freely giving without consideration of return. The essence of Agamemnon, on the other hand, is to calculate carefully in advance what one expects to get in return before one agrees to give anything. For Rank a person who is pulled too much by possibility is one who has bitten off too big a chunk of life, who does not partialize enough. A person who is dragged down too much by necessity is, in contrast, one who has bitten off too small a chunk of life, who partializes too much. Rosenzweig's Abraham bites off too big a chunk of life. That person does not partialize enough in demanding no account of what will be received in return for unqualified giving. Rosenzweig's Agamemnon bites off too small a chunk of life, partializing too much in demanding a complete account in advance of what will be received. This is the dichotomy shared by Rosenzweig and Rank.

A comparison of Buber and Horney further deepens this parallel. In Buber's I-Thou relation, the "thou" is known directly, as an end in itself; in his I-it relation, the "it" is perceived indirectly, as a means to an end. For Horney a self-effacing solution to neurosis involves a complete longing for a total surrendering love; an expansive solution involves an attempt to manipulate and control others in order to gain mastery over them. Buber's I-thou relation, by the very nature of its whole surrender to the other as end, potentially contains aspects of Horney's self-effacing solution to neurosis. Buber's I-it relation, by the nature of its push toward mastery of the other as means, contains aspects of Horney's expansive solution to neurosis.

What then do we actually have after drawing these parallels? On the one hand we have Shestov, Rosenzweig, and Buber; on the other, Becker, Rank, and Horney. Shestov's "leaping Abraham," Rosenzweig's "selfless Abraham," and Buber's "thou as end" are compared respectively to Becker's "overconcern with necessity," Rank's "overpartializer," and Horney's "expander." The two lines of thought are different in emphasis, yet they share a common thread. To put it succinctly, the "covenant" realtor for Shestov, Rosenzweig, and Buber is the potential schizophrenic for Becker, Rank, and Horney. The "contract" realtor for Shestov, Rosenzweig, and Buber is the potential depressive for Becker, Rank, and Horney.

The religious writers emphasize potential for direct interpersonal commitment, whereas the psychological writers emphasize potential for indirect intrapersonal psychosis. Nevertheless, the parallels emerge around epistemological bias and must be pointed out. The covenant relator and the potential schizophrenic both leap before they look, in that they bite off too big a chunk of life, being too naive in throwing necessity to the wind. The contract relator and the potential depressive both look before they leap, in that they bite off too small a chunk of life, being too calculating and cautious in ignoring possibility. The theoretical issue of how these two very different life orientations may be resolved by persons in their ongoing relationships will now be explored.

CHAPTER 3

Interpersonal Distancing Styles in Hellenic and Hebraic Personalities: On Reconciling Possibility and Necessity

The question of how people reconcile covenant and contract, or alternatively, possibility and necessity, in their ongoing relationships is not an easy one. Yet they do—and how they do seems to be a very important issue. It is the purpose of this chapter to employ the psychological theory of affiliative conflict (Argyle and Dean, 1965) to delineate the Hellenic versus Hebraic personality styles with regard to interpersonal distancing.

Conflict Theory

The theory of affiliative conflict derives from the classic laboratory work on conflict done by Neal Miller and his associates (1944). Their paradigm was as follows: A rat was allowed to run down a straight runway to a goal region, at which were food pellets and/or an electric grid. Pushes toward (approach) and pulls away (avoidance) from the goal region at each point along the runway were recorded and calibrated by means of a shoulder harness. The results demonstrate that the avoidance tendencies increase with closeness to the goal region more quickly than do the approach tendencies. In other words, the avoidance gradient is steeper than approach (Figure 1a).

The meaning of this finding is that there exists an equilibrium point (E_1) for the rat with regard to the goal region, past which it will not go. There the rat will be pushed back as the avoidance forces dominate its approach. Yet if the rat is too far from the goal, approach forces will dominate and pull the rat to equilibrium. While it is true that the heights of the approach and avoidance gradients may vary with the respective strengths of the appetitive and aversive stimuli, the relative slopes should remain invariant. Thus there will always be a stable equilibrium; the only question will be its exact location on the runway. With increases in the strength of the appetitive as compared to the aversive stimuli, the equilibrium point will move closer to the goal region (E_2). With greater increases in the strength of the aversive stimuli, the equilibrium point will move farther from the goal region (E_3).

Figure 1

Two Types of Conflict Structures

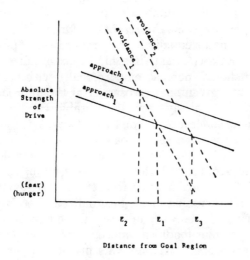

FIGURE 1a: Conflict Curves—Avoidance Steeper than Approach

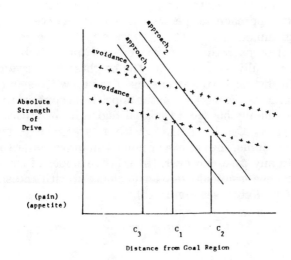

FIGURE 1b: Conflict Curves—Approach Steeper than Avoidance

However, more recent thinking by Miller (1959) and Kelman (1962), suggests that this pattern may not always obtain; that in fact there may well be cases where approach is steeper than avoidance. Their reasoning is as follows: In the classic experiments, hunger was employed as the appetitive stimulus, and, fear was used as the aversive stimulus. Hunger, as such, represents a largely internalized drive source—the rat remains equally hungry regardless of proximity to the food pellets. Fear, in contrast, is a highly externalized drive source —the rat's fear should increase monotonically with proximity to the electric grid. Thus, given some crossover of the approach and avoidance gradients, there always will be a stable equilibrium; the only question will be its exact location on the runway. With increases in the strength of the appetitive as compared to the aversive stimuli, the equilibrium point will move closer to the goal region (E_2). With greater increases in the strength of the aversive stimuli, in contrast, the equilibrium point will move farther from the goal region (E_3).[3]

It would follow then that if an internalized aversive source (e.g., sustained pain) was paired with an externalized appetitive source (e.g., appetite for a particular food), the approach gradient might well prove to have a steeper slope. Although this prediction per se has to our knowledge not been tested, the effects of fear have been compared with pain (Miller 1959), showing a much steeper slope for the former. It thus seems quite probable that the curve presented in Figure 1b can obtain; that is, approach can be steeper than avoidance.[4]

Unlike the "avoidance steeper than approach" curve presented in Figure 1a, the "approach steeper than avoidance" curve does not allow for an equilibrium other than at the exact crossover point (C_1). Moves in either direction push the rat to extremes, either totally toward the goal region or totally away from it. The heights of the two gradients will vary with the respective strengths of the appetitive and aversive stimuli. The greater the increase in the appetite as opposed to the aversive stimulus, the farther from the goal region is the crossover point for total closeness (C_2). In contrast, with greater relative increase in the aversive stimulus, the crossover point will move closer to the goal region (C_3). In any case, however, the relative slopes of the approach and the avoidance gradients remain unchanged with the shifting of their respective heights (see Figure 1b).

The Psychology of Interpersonal Distancing:
Compensation versus Reciprocity

The previous analysis has direct implications for the psychology of interpersonal distancing; that is, the manner in which one person approaches or avoids another. Two major models have emerged to explain the empirical patterns. The first is the "distance equilibrium" or compensation model of Argyle and Dean (1965); the second is the model of reciprocity of Jourard (1971).

The compensation model has been derived from the work on nonverbal distancing behaviors (e.g., eye contact, physical distance, touching) and suggests that any move away from the equilibrium distance between two people (whether too near or too far) will be met by compensatory moves to restore the original distance level. In other words, approach will evoke avoidance and avoidance will evoke approach. This finding has been supported in a considerable number of nonverbal studies (Aiello, 1972; Clore, 1969; Goldberg, Kiesler, and Collins, 1969; McAdoo, 1963; Mehrabian and Diamond, 1971; Patterson, Mullins, and Romano, 1971; Sommer, 1968; Watson and Graves, 1966).

The reciprocity model, in contrast, derives from research on verbal distancing behaviors (e.g., length and intimacy of verbal disclosure) and suggests that any move away from the equilibrium distance between two people will be met by further moves in the same direction. In other words, approach will evoke further approach and avoidance further avoidance. This effect has emerged in a number of studies on verbal reciprocity (Ehrlich and Graven, 1971; Jourard, 1971; Koplan, Firestone, Klein and Sodikoff, 1983; Levinger and Senn, 1967; Tognoli, 1969; Worthy, Gary, and Kahn, 1969).

It should be fairly clear at this point that a one-to-one parallelism exists between the two varieties of the conflict curve and the two modes of interpersonal distancing. The compensation hypothesis derives from the "avoidance steeper than approach" model, whereas the reciprocity hypothesis derives from "approach steeper than avoidance" (Firestone, 1977).

Hellenic Versus Hebraic Personality Styles

The difference between Hellenic and Hebraic personality styles can be diagrammed in exactly the terms outlined above. This particular dichotomy has reverberated through the centuries and has been treated by such distinguished thinkers as Matthew Arnold, Leo Baeck, William Barrett, Thorleif Boman, Martin Buber, Harvey Cox, Israel Efros, Samson Raphael Hirsch, Horace Kallen, Ludwig Lewisohn, Thomas Mann, Reinhold Niebuhr, Maurice Samuel, Lev Shestov, and Milton Steinberg. With the exception of Arnold, a fairly consistent implicit view of two opposing personality styles emerges. The Hellenic is stable; the Hebraic is open. The Hellenic is static; the Hebraic is dynamic. The Hellenic is geometric; the Hebraic is historical. In conflict terms the Hellenic personality can be viewed as possessing an abstract idealism with concrete situational realities puncturing this optimism. As such, it corresponds to the "hunger-fear" paradigm and the "avoidance steeper than approach" outcome.

From the perspective of the thinkers mentioned above, the Hebraic personality can be viewed as eschewing the abstract and becoming alive to the particular situational encounter. As such, it corresponds to the "appetite-pain" paradigm and the "approach steeper than avoidance" outcome. The Hellenic personality can thus be viewed as a compensating personality and the Hebraic as a reciprocating one. In other words, the Hellenic personality can be seen as having a static equilibrium point where the approach and avoidance curves cross. The Hebraic personality, on the other hand, has no static equilibrium.

In this theoretical position, as diagrammed in Figure 2, the Hellenic personality contains two poles. At the "far" first pole (b), the Hellenic personality is in an area where approach dominates avoidance and can view the world positively in the manner of a European humanist (e.g., humanity is wonderful). However, this positive orientation emerges only at a distance. When this personality type is confronted with close contact, (a) it reverts to the negativity of a Stoic (e.g., close relations are a hassle). In like manner the Hebraic personality can be divided into two poles. At a distance, the negative pole (c) is displayed, that of an Ecclesiastic (e.g., the world is vain). However, this pole is replaced at closer contact (d) by the positive orientation of the Hebrew humanist (e.g., to save one life is to save the world). (See Buber on the contrasts between I-it and I-thou relations: Buber [1958] 1970; and European and Hebrew humanism: Buber (1949] 1973).

Covenant versus Contract

Of particular interest to the covenant-contract problem as developed by Shestov and, indirectly by Becker, are the tiers of translation, developed in Chapter 2, of these two lines of thinking with regard to approach-avoidance theory or, alternatively, "interpersonal distancing." First, the twin issues of perception and motivation seem to translate nicely some of the thinking of Rank and Rosenzweig. Second, the delineation of alternate epistemological positions seems to capture some of the thinking of Buber and Horney. Of course, all these issues are in reality quite interconnected to the dichotomy between Shestov and Becker. We are trying to segment them artificially to achieve some clarity of understanding. It is instructive to explore these interrelationships further, all the while keeping in the back of our minds the problem to which we shall return, that of deepening our understanding of covenantal versus pathological relations.

Perhaps the common point of departure for Rosenzweig and Rank is their emphasis on the fear of death. They take this, respectively, into

Figure 2

A Delineation of Hellenic versus Hebraic

Personalities in Conflict Terms

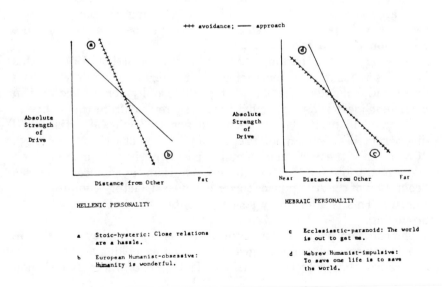

different psychological domains—Rosenzweig to the area of cognition-perception, and Rank to the area of motivation. However, they both deal with the issue of approach-avoidance.

This point is more directly illustrated in the writings of Rank. Rank ([1932]1968) describes two needs that must be reconciled in the human being—the need for separation (will) and the need for union (love), or to put it in conflict terms, the avoidance drive and the approach drive. Rank further describes two fears that must be mastered in order to develop a creative and constructive rapprochement between freedom and love. The first fear that must be mastered is the life fear (the fear of separation). This life fear is counterbalanced by a death fear. The anxiety over separation tends to preserve union, but the fear of passive dependence (the death fear) tends to activate the drive of the will toward separation. Both this fear of life or separation (i.e., avoidance fear) and this fear of death or union (i.e., approach fear) must be mastered in order to develop a creative integration of these two basic life forces.

One may apply Rank's formulation to an understanding of the Hebraic and Hellenic conflict structures in terms of alternate ways of resolving the life fear and the death fear. In the Hellenic structure, avoidance is steeper than approach, and a point of midway distance in a relationship is achieved, allowing neither satisfactory union nor separation. Here, at best, the life fears and the death fears are compromised, with neither being totally resolved. In the Hebraic structure, approach is steeper than avoidance, allowing free union and free separation. This kind of relation thus demands a more complete resolution of life fears and death fears.

Consider now the thinking of Franz Rosenzweig ([1930] 1971) on this issue. Its translation to approach-avoidance terms is certainly more indirect and demands a mediating step. Philosophy, for Rosenzweig, in particular idealistic philosophy, tends to "retreat from the reality of the person in particular to people in general" (cf. Allport's [1937] distinction between an idiographic and a nomothetic psychology). "Cognition of the particular" simultaneously pushes toward free union and separation (i.e., approach steeper than avoidance), whereas "cognition of the All" pushes toward an unsatisfactory compromise of the two. This is admittedly speculative, but the line of argument is promising.

The common point of departure for Buber and Horney is their emphasis on a total all-embracing surrender versus looking at the other in a more calculating objective fashion. The mode of orientation (I-thou versus I-it; self-effacing versus expansive solutions) determines that of committing (covenant versus contract), knowing (direct versus indirect), perceiving (whole versus part), and purpose (ends versus means).

This too can be applied to our initial formulations of Hebraic and Hellenic conflict structures. In other words, Buber's I-thou and Horney's self-effacing solution to neurosis may both map into an "approach steeper than avoidance" structure. Buber's I-it and Horney's expansive solution to neurosis, in contrast, may both map into an "avoidance steeper than approach" structure.

A Redefinition of Covenant

The discerning reader has probably sensed a pathology in both sides of the many polarities discussed above. Greek thought reflects this pathology, separating rational and emotional aspects of life into polarized entities (the Apollonian and Dionysian subcultures). Judaic thought, however, attempts to synthesize what many of the above-mentioned thinkers call covenantal contract. Judaism accepts certain absolute values and seeks to apply and carry them out. For Abraham there is neither contradiction nor separation between his covenant with God and his contractual argument with God to try to save the people of Sodom and Gomorrah. Indeed one demands the other.

This latter part is extremely crucial in correcting historical misconceptions of Judaism. Pharisaic Judaism is interpreted as obsessive legalism (i.e., only contract). We are arguing that Pharisaic Judaism represented a series of contractual arrangements making manifest the covenant. Walter Kaufmann's (1976) discussion of Pauline Christology is quite instructive here.

> The heart of Paul's message is a verse in one of the minor prophets of the Hebrew Bible, Habakkuk, whose brief book comprises only three short chapters. In the original language and context, the meaning of verse 4 of chapter 2 is none too clear, but Paul's version of it is not startling: "the just man shall live by faith" (Romans 1:17 and Galatians 3:11). In Hebrew, *emunah* meant firmness, truthfulness, reliability, faithfulness, not belief that anything was the case or had happened.[5] But among the Jews of Paul's time far bolder exegeses were not uncommon; and this last half of a verse in a very minor prophet became for Paul the epitome of his kerygma. Of course, Habakkuk was not suggesting any opposition between law and faith, between doing and believing, but Paul evidently had not derived his doctrine fro

Habakkuk; he merely found in him a convenient proof text. (Kaufmann, 1976, p. 130)

These are strong words with implications far beyond our present scope. They indicate that any attempt to segment off covenant (and possibility) from contract (and necessity) produces disastrous results. It is also interesting to note in this regard that Kaufmann has continually emphasized the need for synthesis of I-thou and I-it in his treatment of Buber (Buber [1958] 1970).

Much the same point has been recently made by the exiled Russian novelist Alexander Solzhenitsyn.

I have spent all my life under a Communist regime, and I will tell you that a society without an objective legal standard is a terrible one indeed. . . . But a society with no other scale but the legal one is not quite worthy of man either. (Solzhenitsyn 1978)

Covenant (and possibility) and contract (and necessity) must be reconciled in real relations. Acts without love are insufficient—but so is love without acts. The Hebraic and Hellenic civilizations provide opposite wisdoms with regard to this reconciliation, the Hebraic integrating covenant and contract and the Hellenic polarizing its culture into Apollonian and Dionysian segments.

A fitting ending to this chapter emerges from the opposition in stances taken by Lev Shestov and Ernest Becker toward the famous dictum of Spinoza: *Non ridere, non lugere, neque detestari, sed intelligere* (Not to laugh, not to lament, not to curse, but to understand). Becker admires Spinoza's dictum as liberating the person from the morass of pure emotion; Shestov despises Spinoza's dictum as enslaving the person into the snare of pure reason.

Any reconciliation of contract and covenant demands the human yet inhuman burden of being able both to understand and simultaneously to laugh and lament. Yet this reconciliation is not easy and must be done with skill. For present purposes it may be said that reason need not negate faith. To laugh and lament—to understand—yet to laugh and lament. The difference between covenantal and narcissistic contracts is the theme of the remainder of this volume.

CHAPTER 4

Man and Woman in the Classical and Biblical Worlds

It is in fashion today for some feminist thinkers to trace modern misogynist tendencies to Judaic origins in general and to the Hebrew Bible in particular. The line of this argument is to portray the New Testament as freeing woman from the patriarchal enslavement of the Jewish Old Testament. It is the intent of this chapter to suggest that much of modern Western misogyny stems from Greek influences that are quite foreign to Judaism.

We will try to illustrate these general themes with two specific comparisons. First, we briefly contrast the respective Greek and Hebrew terms for womb: *hystera* and *rehem*. Second, we examine at greater length the respective Greek and Hebrew accounts of the first woman: *Pandora* and *Eve*.

Hystera versus Rehem: The Function of the Womb

Consider Milton Himmelfarb's (1973) etymological analysis of the Greek and Hebrew terms for womb in his book *The Jews of Modernity*. Himmelfarb distinguishes the Greek term for womb, *hystera*, from the Hebrew term, *rehem*. From *hystera* come terms like "hysterectomy" and the modern psychiatric term "hysteria," literally the disease of the "wandering uterus." (Plato, *Timaeus,* 91). The Hebrew *rehem* shares a common root with words such as *rahamim,* meaning pity and compassion. Himmelfarb sums his etymological point thus: "Hellenically, the womb generates hysteria . . . Hebraically, the womb generates pity. Hellenism has something antiwoman, antiwomanly, misogynist and so has our culture, high or low, under Apollo's sign or Dionysus'!" (Himmelfarb 1973, 303; also see Ellis, 1903, volume 1, p. 210)

Hysteria and the Greek View of Woman:
Some Illustrations from Psychology.

Let us examine this last point in more detail through analysis of the way in which hysteria was viewed in the Greek world and its connection to the way in which women were viewed. The ancient Greeks (see Plato, *Timaeus*, 91) believed that certain hysterical physical symptoms in women were actually caused by a wandering or displacement of the uterus. This type of hysteria was considered more likely to affect widows and virgins than married women. Hysteria generally was thought to involve physical symptoms such as shortness of breath, pains in the chest, lumps in the throat, pain in the groin and legs, instances of fainting, and seizures. Psychological symptoms generally involved mass dissociative phenomena and inability to focus on a particular problem.

Bennett Simon (1978) puts it this way in *Mind and Madness in Ancient Greece*:

> The hysterical character, usually a woman, tends to be histrionic and represses and ignores much important social interaction, particularly in the sphere of sexuality. This kind of patient does not frequently consult medical doctors about specific somatic complaints. If she seeks psychiatric help, she most often complains of inability to get along with people or to be successful in love. The frequency of minor hysterical conversion symptoms is probably higher than normal in such patients, though the data is not altogether clear. *In recent years it has been pointed out that the "hysterical character" may well be a man's version of what women are like in general.* (p. 240).

Consideration of the Greek prescriptions for treatment of hysteria is instructive as well.

> Treatments varied with symptoms, but commonly involved bandaging (to prevent further ascension of the uterus), orally administering medicaments (wine, for example), fetid fumigations to the nose (to repel the ascendent uterus), and aromatic fumigations inserted in the vagina (to attract the wandering uterus back to its proper place). Marriage (or remarriage), intercourse, and procreation were prescribed for victims who were virgins or widows. (p. 243)

Even more pertinent are records of Dionysian rituals performed by Greek women who left their homes and went into the woods to reenact the frenzy of Maenadism. Maenads were wild women traveling seminude through the woods and practicing the *sparagmos* and *omophagia* (tearing apart and eating raw) of an animal or human. Euripides' tragedy, *The Bacchae*, portrays the conflict between the repressed overintellectualized male Pentheus and the god of the Maenads, Dionysus. In a dramatic series of three encounters,

Dionysus is portrayed as leading Pentheus to a bloody dismemberment at the hands of the Maenads and Pentheus' own mother, Agave (Kraemer, 1980).

Generally, it can be argued that the Greek male dichotomized his personality into intellect versus emotion, rejected emotion, and projected it onto the female. He thus feared contact with her and viewed her as mad, specifically hysteric. He tried to control her rigidly because of his obsessive attempts to avoid his own feminine side. The Greek female had to break with the society in order to express, in distorted form, feminine emotional life. Simon suggests that Dionysian ritual and myth served some of the same purposes as hysterical illness and its treatment, through providing a means of expressing and redressing serious social and psychological imbalances between the sexes not available in the main society.

Rahamim and the Hebrew View of Woman: Some Illustrations from Psychology

The case in the Hebrew world is diametrically different. Man most definitely does not run away from his compassionate side. David Bakan (1979) argues that the Hebrew Bible provides a "written constitution for family life in western civilization" in his book *And They Took Themselves Wives*. Specifically the Bible shows males involved in the responsibilities of caring for children.

> Thus the Bible may also be regarded as expressing what may be considered as the effeminization of the man. In coming to share the care of children, he came to share in the archaic functions of the female. In coming to understand that he was biologically connected with children, he became like a mother. Indeed, even such super-masculine traits as are associated with being a warrior may be seen as outgrowths of a mother's protectiveness with respect to her children. In this sense, paternalization is equally maternalization of the male. (Bakan, p. 14)

Much the same insight, though opposite emotional reaction, emerges from Spinoza's violent attacks on Judaism (see Franck, 1979) Spinoza deprecates compassion (*rehem*), which he termed *muliebris misericordia* or "womanish pity" (Spinoza, 1955, Volume II, p. 126). This reveals Spinoza's contempt for both women and Judaism and is probably a component in Judaism's rejection and excommunication of Spinoza. S. D. Luzzatto condemns Spinoza on exactly these grounds and views the Spinoza ethical system as being "Attic" rather than

Jewish—i.e., detached and disconnected from compassion rather than committed (see Rosenbloom, 1965).

A similar analysis has emerged in Carol Gilligan's contemporary critique of the Kohlberg Moral Development Scheme as being appropriate for women. Gilligan (1978) suggests that

> the arc of developmental theory leads from infantile dependence to adult autonomy, tracing a path characterized by an increasing differentiation of self from other [which is good] and a progressive freeing of thought from contextual constraints [which is bad]. [Insertions ours]. The individual, meeting fully the developmental challenges of adolescence as set for him by Piaget, Erikson, and Kohlberg, thinks formally, proceeding from theory to fact, and defines both the self and the moral autonomously. . . . Yet the men whose theories have largely informed this understanding of development have all been plagued by the same problem, the problem of women, whose sexuality remains more diffuse, whose perception of self is so much more tenaciously embedded in relationships with others and whose moral dilemmas hold them in a mode of judgment that is insistently contextual. The solution has been to consider women as either deviant or deficient in their development (pp. 481, 482).

Pandora versus Eve: The Entrance of Woman

Let us now consider the respective "first woman" accounts in the Greek and Hebrew civilizations: that of Pandora and that of Eve.

The popular version of the Pandora myth can be found in Hesiod and has been summarized by Lachs (1974).

> After Prometheus had stolen the heavenly fire and had given it to mortals, Zeus punished him by chaining him to a mountain where an eagle tore at his liver by day: it grew back every night so that the torture might be repeated the following day. But Zeus was not satisfied with this: He wanted more revenge. He commanded Hephaestus to fashion a woman out of clay and ordered the gods to bestow upon her choicest gifts. Hephaestus gave her a human voice, Aphrodite gave her beauty and the power of seduction, Athene taught her needlework, and Hermes gave her cunning and the art of flattery. She became the first woman, and the most beautiful one, Pandora (all-giving or all-gifted). She was, however, also by the will of Zeus, made deceitful and mischievous, the first of a line of such women. Zeus than sent her to Epimetheus, the brother of Prometheus, to become his wife. Epimetheus was warned by his brother not to accept any gift from Zeus, but he did not heed this advice and he married Pandora. Epimetheus had in his house a jar containing all kinds of miseries—Old Age, Labor and Sickness. Pandora,

out of curiosity, opened the jar and released all the evils contained therein. Hope, however, remained under the rim of the jar, and fortunately the lid was shut before it escaped. (pp. 341–342)

The story of Eve in Genesis is somewhat longer and almost too well known to repeat. Nevertheless, we will briefly summarize it for the point of comparison.

On the sixth day, God formed man from dust, in His own likeness, and gave to him dominion over all living things. He placed him in Eden, a paradisal garden pleasant to the sight and good for food. But God was displeased that amongst all living creatures, man was still alone and therefore created for him a helpmeet. God removed a rib from Adam, the man, while he was sleeping and formed it into a woman. Upon awaking, Adam exclaimed that she should be called "woman" because she was taken "out of man." Adam and his wife were unashamed to be naked before each other. God permitted Adam and his wife the full freedom of Eden that they might work and keep it. Of the Tree of Knowledge alone, He commanded that they neither eat nor touch it lest they surely die. The serpent who was in the garden subtly tricked the woman into eating of the forbidden fruit, and she convinced Adam to do likewise. When they had done so, they were ashamed for the first time of their own nakedness and hid from the sight of the Lord. God knew and questioned Adam who replied that the woman had given him the fruit. She, in turn, placed the blame on the serpent. God cursed the serpent to crawl on its belly forever and set a lasting enmity between its offspring and that of woman. God told the woman that henceforth she would be ruled by her husband and bring forth children in pain. Finally God caused Adam to know the toil of the field all the days of his life and, upon his death, to return to the dust from which he was formed. God then made garments of skin for Adam and his wife who was now called Eve because she was to be the mother of all living things, and cast him from Eden lest he become like God in his knowledge of Good and Evil and thus eat of the fruit hanging on the tree of life and live forever.

The question arises as to how these two stories are to be viewed in relationship to each other. One line of interpretation among Old Testament scholars is to stress the parallel structure of the two stories.

In the Bible, God warns Adam not to eat of the fruit of the tree; in the Pandora myth, Prometheus warns his brother Epimetheus not to accept any gifts from Zeus. Eve, the first woman, is called the mother of all life; Pandora, also the first woman, is created out of clay, and it is said, from her is the race of women and female kind. Eve, tempted by the serpent, causes her own and her husband's banishment and brings ills upon

mankind, while Pandora, prompted by curiosity, brings misfortunes
upon herself, her husband, and all mortals (Lachs 1974, p. 343).

Graves and Patai follow this thinking in suggesting that the Hebrew
Bible parallels Greek myth in gradually *reducing* women from sacred
beings to chattels. "The Greeks made woman responsible for man's
unhappy lot by adopting Hesiod's fable of Pandora's jar, from which a
Titan's foolish wife let loose the combined spites of sickness, old age
and vice . . . "Similarly Jehovah punishes Eve for causing the Fall of
Man" (p. 15).

Most recent sociohistorical work agrees with the above assessment
with regard to the Greek woman (cf. Pomeroy, 1975; Simon, 1978;
Slater, 1968). With regard to the Hebrew woman, however, opinion is
more varied (cf. Bakan, 1979; Koltun, 1976; Maertens, 1969). For us, it
is clear that the biblical woman maintains considerable dignity, and
there is an alternative way of comparing the Pandora and Eve stories.

Pandora and the Greek Woman: Some Illustrations from Mythology

Pandora seems to represent a *curse* to man, sent specifically by Zeus
as a punishment for Prometheus having previously attempted to gain
independence from Zeus (through the stealing of fire). In Maerten's
terms, woman is initially seen as the "mysterious other" closely associated with the capriciousness of nature. As man attempts to free himself from nature and gain some control over it, he comes to attempt to
dominate and control woman (Maertens, 1969, pp. 44, 45). Woman,
says the Pandora myth, is a "race apart." She (Pandora) is created out
of clay; *from her is the race of woman and female kind.*

Such polarization between man and woman fills the pages of Greek
myth and literature. Man was rational and controlled, in short the very
symbol of *logos.* Woman, on the other hand, was man's antithesis; she
was irrational, uncontrolled—in short the other, the symbol of *eros.*
The ancient Greek masculine mind seemed to repress all that was ob-
jectionable to him in himself and projected it onto woman—thus,
Tyche, Maenads, furies, evil Sphinxes, Medusas, harpies, and witches,
such as Hecate and Medea. Nietzsche (1956) in fact has argued that
the polarization between man and woman is the essence of Greek
tragedy.

Two mythical exceptions to this polarization seem to stand
out—Athena and Dionysus. Athena, the masculinized woman, was

born from the *head* of Zeus; Dionysus, the feminized man, was born from his *thigh*. But these exceptions only serve to prove the rule. Although it is true that some women may have consciously chosen to model themselves after Athena and some men after Dionysus, Athena represented far ˉmore a masculine prototype (of the trustworthy woman) and Dionysus a feminine one. Sophocles' *Antigone,* for example, contrasts the meek Ismene with her highly principled and willful sister, Antigone.

Eve and the Hebrew Woman: Some Illustrations from the Bible

The Genesis account, in contrast, presents Eve as a *helpmeet* to Adam. Nevertheless, she actively pushes him to disobey God (by eating of the forbidden fruit of the tree of knowledge), and it has been objected that Eve is punished for this action by subservience to her husband: "Yet your urge shall be for your husband, and he shall rule over you" (Gen. 3:16).

Jewish tradition, however, rejects this interpretation. According to Rashi, for example, this verse indicates merely that it will be considered proper for a man to ask directly for sexual intercourse, while propriety requires woman to be less direct (Rashi, Gen. 3:16).

The Hebrew Bible, in fact, offers a long list of nonsubservient women. Certainly Sarah and Rebecca exhibit power in their marriages in their successful interventions into the inheritance process. In addition, Miriam, the daughters of Zelophahad, Deborah, Abigail, the woman of Abela, the woman of Shunem, Bathsheba, Michal, Hulda, Ruth, and Esther all provide examples of independent women who, far from abandoning their femininity, use intelligence and courage in traditional roles. A reciprocal nonsubservient relationship between man and woman seems very much the rule—where each belongs to the other. "I am my beloved's and my beloved is mine" (Song of Songs, 6:3).

The modern obsession with career, for *both* man and woman, does not seem, in the context of antiquity, as prerequisite or as a substitute for a strong sense of self. At the same time Eve is not seen as the mysterious other. In the creation story she is portrayed not as coming from the clay, as does Pandora (and Lilith, by some accounts), but from Adam's own body. She is portrayed not as coming from his head (as is Athena) or his thigh (as is Dionysus) but from what common translation calls his rib. She is not a curse, but a helpmeet; she arrives before the pivotal act (eating of the forbidden fruit) rather than after (Prometheus' stealing of fire). Nor is she portrayed as a race apart, being given the name Eve—*mother of all living things.* Probably woman receives this name only *after* she and Adam have eaten the fruit of the forbidden tree (see Table 1).

Christian, Psychoanalytic, and Jewish Views of Eve

In this section we pursue the following strategy: to compare Christian, psychoanalytic, and Jewish views of Eve, examining the degree to which each of those positions seems to confuse Eve with Pandora.

Church Fathers, at times, seem to have assimilated Eve and Pandora (Lachs, 1974) and to have viewed Biblical woman through a prism of Hellenism (see Horowitz, 1979). The story of Eve represents the pivotal foundation myth of Pauline Christology. Eating of the forbidden fruit is not only sin but *original sin,* which leads to the fall of man from an initial state of innocence and grace.[6]

The result of Eve's action for Christians is that the human race is condemned to live outside the miraculous garden until the risen Christ

Table 1

A Summary of Characteristics of

Pandora versus Eve

	Pandora	Eve
origin	clay	Adam's rib
time of arrival	*after* man has stolen fire	*before* man has eaten of the forbidden fruit
description	punishment	helpmeet
descendants	mother of the race of women and female kind	mother of all life

redeems them from their sinfulness. Indeed, he is described by Paul as the "Second Adam." What Christ's resurrection gives to the believing Christian, in this view, is a return to the state of innocence, oneness, and even "life everlasting" existence in the garden. (I Cor. 15:22, 45) The original relationship between the Deity and man is thus renewed. If Christ is the "Second Adam," Mary is the "Second Eve." The weakness and sensuality of Eve and her daughters will be supplanted by the purity of the Virgin Mary, presumably the state of woman before the fall.

Building on this approach, psychoanalysis generally supports a different comparison of Pandora and Eve. Some Christian thinking correlates the fruit of the tree of knowledge either with Pandora herself (i.e., both are forbidden or warned against it) or with the jar or box in Epimetheus' house (i.e., both contain mysteries which better remain unopened). As such, Eve and Pandora seem to emerge with the same taint—untrustworthy, overcurious, and perhaps even forbidden to begin with (cf. Lachs 1974, pp. 341–342).

Erich Fromm (1966) offers a different line of argument based on psychoanalytic thinking. The state in Eden represents a symbiotic fusion typical of infancy. Eating of the tree, though a disobedient act, allows for the beginning of human history. Under this view Eve seemingly becomes a blessing, pushing Adam to achieve autonomy and *sharing* it with him. This suggests a different juxtaposition of the Eve and Pandora stories: that between the fruit of the tree of knowledge and the heavenly fire which Prometheus himself has stolen from Zeus. Both the tree of knowledge and fire may represent autonomous knowledge through which man may free himself from a total dependency on the Godhead, whether God or Zeus. Here, very different roles seem to emerge: Eve is a helpmeet and Pandora a punishment.

Generally, the rabbinic literature views woman as the *supporter* and *helpmeet* of man, not as a *curse* or a *punishment*. It is the man more than the woman who faces directly the intellectual challenge of the relationship with God, both in the garden and after. Yet almost all commentators see the women's role as highly positive and important. Kli Yakar (Mikraot Gedolot) and Abravanel are the most emphatic as to the damage that a poorly motivated woman can wreak upon her husband's spiritual welfare. The rabbinic view with regard to Eve is that the man and woman together foolishly chose to surrender a productive way of life and a close relationship with God in Eden for the sake of illusory ego needs. Their new life outside the garden is centered in work and struggle toward rebuilding that relationship. The basic tension in the human existence is whether both men and women will continue to be ruled by their illusory ego needs or will work to follow God's commands in an ever-deepening relationship with Him.

A number of somewhat varying interpretations are offered by the rabbinic commentators, but the basic themes are essentially the same:

1. It is agreed that Adam and Eve had conjugal relations in Eden before eating the fruit (e.g., Genesis. Rabbah, 18:10, 22:3; Rashi, Gen. 3:1; Ramban, Gen. 2:9; Sforno, Gen. 3:7) Now, these relations became a source of shame because the people no longer used them in the divine service but only for their own pleasure.

2. The garden is not seen as a magical land where man lived an idyllic and innocent existence. The man did have to work, although, according to some, not as hard as his descendants (Berlin, Gen., 2:8-9; Ramban, Gen. 2:8).

3. Nor was there anything magical about the fruit of the tree of knowledge. The change in man emerged as a result of a decision to subordinate God's command to his own values and needs. The prohibition on the tree of knowledge was not the only one placed on man. However, it can be argued that it was the only (hoq) statute, the sole law whose benefits were not apparent to man and which would have to be kept only for love of God (Hirsch, Gen. 2:16).

4. There is no sense of deep-seated conflict between man and woman. Nor are Adam and Eve necessarily to be seen as prototypes of their sexes. They are individuals. Another man and woman might have reacted differently in their situation. Thus there is no original sin. Nothing that the man and woman did removes or limits the power of their descendants to decide between right and wrong for themselves. Every individual must work out his own relationship with God (Hirsch, Gen. 3:9).

5. Finally, the rabbis do not blame the woman alone for the fall from Eden. In fact, the Midrash criticizes Adam for trying to pass the buck to Eve and for seeming ungrateful to God for the precious gift of the woman (Rashi, Genesis 3:12). God Himself had dressed Eve in great beauty for her first meeting with Adam and had blessed them at their wedding (Genesis Rabbah, 18:1; Talmud, *Eruvin*, 18b). In fact a well-known midrash (Genesis Rabbah 19:12) states that the main reason for which the man and woman were driven from the garden was that they each attempted to blame someone else for the sin (Eve blamed the serpent, and Adam blamed Eve).

Summary

Let us, in summary, return to our major theme. In the West, Eve is a curse, like Pandora, leading man to estrangement from God. Redemption occurs through overturning this primal curse and, in the process, woman's influence (Mary notwithstanding). For Judaism, Eve is a helpmeet, sharing man's estrangement with him. Redemption occurs in passing through the fires of estrangement to a mature reconciliation. Much of the misogyny in present-day Western attitudes toward the Bible seems to come from Greek lenses rather than Jewish origins.

Ultimately, then, this chapter is as much about men and their attitude toward women as it is about women themselves. If men are afraid to show compassion (rahamim), they brutalize their encounters with women, as in the Greek society, and force women to repress their natures or express them in distorted form inside (hysteria) or outside (maenadism) society. If men accept their compassionate side, they encourage the full expression of women's individual natures, as in the Jewish conception of society and family. Men grow in compassion through their own involvement in the processes of family and child care. To the extent that they are ambivalent about their heritage, the attitudes of Western men toward women may waver between these alternatives: (1) The Greek—vacillation between acceptance and fusion of the masculinized woman (e.g. Athena) and polarization, rejection, and even expulsion of the unbridled woman (e.g., Dionysian maenads); or (2) the Jewish—acceptance of the woman as a strong personality within the family (e.g., the Matriarchs).

CHAPTER 5

A Bidimensional Reformulation of Hellenic versus Hebraic Personalities

Chapters 2 through 4 have focused on different neurotic styles, distancing patterns, and gender stereotypes in Greek and Hebrew thought. The present chapter attempts to bidimensionalize these views as an alternative to the often-strained dialectic resolutions of such problems. It sets the stage for a careful comparison of narcissistic and covenantal orientations toward relationships.

A Theoretical Reformulation of Distancing and Gender

A Bidimensional Approach to Interpersonal Distancing

Our first reformulation bidimensionalizes the established un-dimensional view of interpersonal distance. This unidimensional view is typified by Minuchin (1974) who views distance as a single bipolar dimension ranging from far or remote distance at one end to near or intimate distance on the other. Minuchin expresses distance in terms of ego boundaries—diffuse ego boundaries leading to *enmeshed* or *embedded* structures on the one hand and rigid boundaries leading to *disengaged* or *isolated* structures on the other. A similar unidimensional view is taken by Lewin (1935) in his analysis of firmness of boundaries (pp. 58–62).

An alternative stance on these issues emerges from the work of Otto Rank (1936). For Rank the "fear of death" (i.e., of being absorbed and overwhelmed) must be resolved independently of the "fear of life" (i.e., of being abandoned or isolated). The near-far continuum may thus be sliced into two dimensions: attachment-detachment and individuation-deindividuation. The first dimension deals with the fear of absorption; the second with the fear of abandonment. An *attached* person has overcome his fear of absorption sufficiently to connect or bond affectionately to another; in other words, to take down the interpersonal *walls*. A *detached* person, in contrast, has failed to overcome this fear and thus is unable to take down the *walls*. An *individuated* person has overcome his fear of abandonment sufficiently to differentiate his self from another; in other words, to evolve healthy self-other *boundaries*.

Journal of Psychology and Judaism, Vol. 8(2), Spring/Summer 1984
© *1984 Human Sciences Press*

A *deindividuated* person, in contrast, has failed to overcome this fear and is thus unable to maintain *boundaries.*

Figure 3 presents this bidimensional view of distance superimposed upon a traditional unidimensional one. What becomes clear is the inherent ambiguity in our traditional (i.e., unidimensional) definitions of near and far. A behavioral tendency toward interpersonal "nearness" (i.e., an approach response) can be seen as potentially containing both a *desire for attachment* and a *fear of individuation.* Likewise, a behavioral tendency toward interpersonal "farness" (i.e., an avoidant response) can be seen as potentially containing both a *desire for individuation* and a *fear of attachment.*

Figure 4 attempts to elaborate this bidimensional view in terms of distancing patterns. Cell B represents a person (*P*) afraid of both abandonment and absorption. As such, he will *compensate* for both the approach and avoidance probes of the other (*O*). In cell D, *P* is afraid of

Figure 3

A Bidimensional View of Interpersonal Distance

Superimposed Upon a Unidimensional One

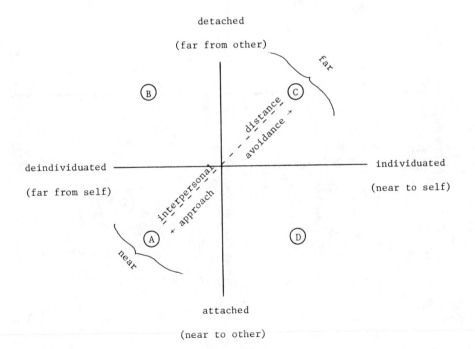

neither abandonment nor absorption. As such he will *reciprocate* both the approach and avoidance probes of *O*. Cell A represents a *P* who has conquered his fear of absorption but not of abandonment. He thus will respond with an *invariant approach* to *O*'s probes *whether* they be approach or avoidance. Finally, cell C represents a *P* who has conquered his fear of abandonment but not fear of absorption. He will respond with an *invariant avoidance* to *O*'s probes, *whether* they be approach or avoidance. Cell E represents a *P* who has conquered his fear of abandonment and absorption to a moderate amount. He will remain

Figure 4

Two Energy Axes

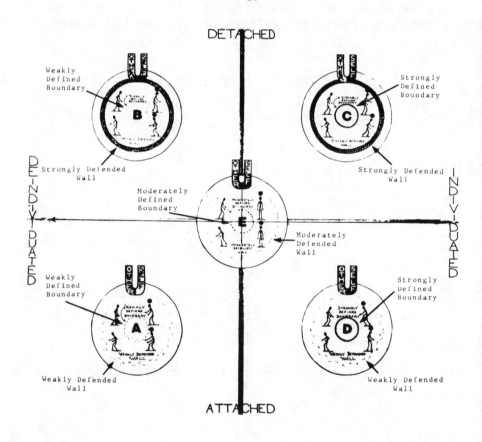

stationary in response to *O*'s probes, *whether* they be approach or avoidance.

A U-tube is drawn at the top of each of the five cells indicating the proportion of energy distributed to self and to other. As can be seen, two axes emerge, operating under opposing energy principles. On the AC axis *a constant amount of energy prevails. The question here is simply the issue of distribution of it to self versus other.* In A, the total energy of *P* is directed outward toward *O* (i.e., *P* is completely other-absorbed). In C, *P* directs his total energy inward, (i.e., *P* is completely self-absorbed). E represents a compromise; the energy is split in half—some kept inward, the other part directed outward. Yet the total energy remains constant, reflecting the Freudian economic constant-energy view. Energy for self becomes available to the extent that it is withdrawn from the other and vice versa.

This is not the case for the BED axis. Here the principles are *an equal amount of energy distribution between self and other* and *a steady increase in the supply of total available energy* from B to E to D. In cell B, *P* has little or no energy to distribute to self or other. In cell E, *P* directs a moderate amount of energy equally between self and other. In cell D, *P* has a great deal of energy which he distributes equally between self and other. This is much more in keeping with Heinz Kohut's (1971) conception of energy distribution.[7]

A Bidimensional Approach to Epistemological Bias

Our second reformulation bidimensionalizes the established view of epistemological bias. Up to this point this paper has viewed epistemological bias as a bipolar dimension ranging from a cognitive or rational orientation on one end to an affective or emotional orientation on the other.

An alternative stance on this issue emerges from the work of Jung (1969) on psychological functions. Jung differentiates four major functions, actually two bipolar pairs. The first pair—thinking versus feeling—represents for Jung rational functions in that they both require an act of judgment. In thinking, one constructs an idea as to what something is. In feeling, one makes judgments as to whether this idea is pleasing or distasteful, beautiful or ugly, exciting or dull. The second pair—sensation versus intuition—represents for Jung irrational functions because they require no reason. Sensation is contingent on the stimuli that are present. Intuition depends on unknown stimuli, a construction going beyond the sensory evidence. Jung defined the four functions very succinctly. *Sensation* (i.e., sense perception) tells us something exists; *thinking* tells us what it is; *feeling* tells us whether it is agreeable or not; and *intuition* tells us whence it comes and where it is going.

Figure 5 presents this bidimensional view of epistemological bias superimposed upon a traditional unidimensional one. What becomes clear is the inherent ambiguity in our traditional (i.e., unidimensional) definitions of affective and cognitive. A bias toward the affective can be seen as containing both a *feeling* and a *sensing* component. A bias toward the cognitive can be seen as containing both an *intuitive* and a *thinking* component.

A Bidimensional Approach to Gender

Our third reformulation has to do with overturning the unidimensional view of gender identity. Up to this point this paper has viewed

Figure 5

A Bidimensional View of Epistemological Bias

Superimposed Upon a Unidimensional One

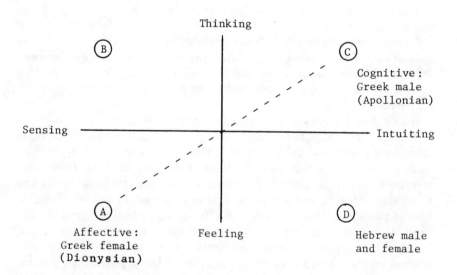

gender identity as a bipolar dimension ranging from a masculine orientation on one end to a feminine one on the other. The masculine orientation involves development of instrumental behavior, assertiveness,
and mature independence, but also passive-aggressive behavior and
physical violence. The feminine orientation, in contrast, involves
development of emotional expressiveness, emotional empathy, and
mature dependency, but also nagging and pressuring (cf. Feldman,
1982b).

An alternative stance on this issue has also been presented in Figure
5. It emerges from the work of Bem (1974, 1975). For Bem,
psychological masculinity and femininity (at least as it has come to be
viewed) can emerge somewhat independently of biological maleness
and femaleness. Further, masculine and feminine characteristics may
occur independently of each other as well. Therefore, a given individual
(whether male or female) can exhibit *only* masculine traits, *only*
feminine traits, *neither* masculine nor *feminine* characteristics, or *both*
masculine *and* feminine characteristics. It is this last condition that
Bem sees as the mark of a balanced individual, one who can combine
within his or her own personality characteristics of intellectuality and
assertiveness with emotionality and empathy.

A Theoretical Reintegration

Culture, Distancing, and Pathology

A bidimensional view of distancing suggests a refining of the earlier
discussed association of compensation with the Greek culture and
reciprocity with the Hebrew culture (see Ch. 3). The critical distinction
between the two cultures may well be the nature of the interweaving
between attachment and individuation. The Greek culture was
polarized into a great duality, labeled by Nietzsche (1956) as that between the Apollonian and Dionysian spirits. The Apollonian spirit was
highly intellectualized, individuated, and detached; the Dionysian
spirit was emotional, deindividuated, and attached. Both these
positions are narcissistic in the Kohutian sense, the first in a mirroring
sense and the second in an idealizing sense (Kohut, 1971) (see also Ch.
7). The Greek world thus seemed unable to integrate attachment and
individuation, offering first one and then the other (see Simon's distinction in this regard between Homer's treatment of the hero in *The
Iliad* and *The Odyssey*, 1978, pp. 58–65) The Hebrew civilization, in
contrast, attempted to integrate the two. This is reflected in the
famous dictum of Hillel. "If I am not for myself, who will be for me? If
I am for myself only, what am I?" (Mishna Avot 1:14).

This readjustment, of course, suggests a reanalysis of the distancing dynamics in the respective cultures. The Greek culture can be seen to vacillate between noncontingent approach or enmeshedness (attachment without individuation) and noncontingent avoidance or isolation (individuation without attachment), the two polarities in Minuchin's (1974) boundary analysis of families. The Hebrew culture, on the other hand, can still be seen as moving toward reciprocity (attachment with individuation). The reanalysis is presented graphically in Figure 6.

The Greek culture can be said to vacillate between hysteria (noncontingent approach) and paranoia (noncontingent avoidance). It is useful in this context to reexamine the etymology of these terms. They both come from Greek words: "paranoia" from *para nous* (other mind) and "hysteria" from *hystera* (womb). Paranoia was literally seen as the fear of invasion by another's mind (in many ways like paranoid schizophrenia today), hysteria was literally seen as the "disease of the wandering uterus." The Hebrew word for womb, in contrast, is *rehem*, from the same root as *rahamim,* the term for pity or compassion (see Ch. 4).

Figure 6

A Bidimensional Reformulation of Hellenic

Versus Hebraic Distancing Styles

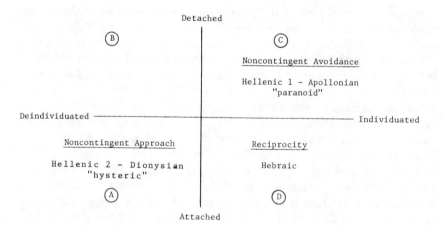

Culture, Gender, and Epistemological Bias

A bidimensional view also suggests a more complicated view of gender differences in epistemological bias than that previously offered. As can be seen in Figure 5, the Greek mind seemed to place the male within the quadrant of *thinking* and *intuiting*. The female, in contrast seems to be placed within the joint cell of *feeling* and *sensing*. It may well be that feeling represents more of a "field dependent" attached orientation than does thinking (cf. Witkin and Goodenough 1977). This would explain the nurturant behaviors associated with women and the aggressive behaviors associated with men. Sensing, on the other hand, may represent a less "sharpened" individuated orientation than does intuiting (cf. Holzman and Gardner 1960). This would explain the greater passivity associated with women and the instrumental orientation associated with men. The legend of Pandora can be seen as reflecting this polarization between male and female orientation. She can be seen as the punishment for man's attempts to achieve autonomy through fire. This oscillation between male and female orientations can be seen as that between an exclusively contractual orientation and one exclusively and covenantal.

For the biblical mind, however, both male and female seem to fall into a quadrant interlocking feeling with intutition (perhaps covenant with contract). The narrative of Eve seems to reflect this nonpolarized view of man and woman. Both men and women seem capable of nurturant and instrumental behavior, and both seem to overcome passivity and aggressiveness. Maturity here seems to reflect not simply a summation of male and female traits but an actual deletion of negative qualities as well.

The above analysis, of course, fits quite well with the discussion of hysteria and paranoia as presented in Figures 5 and 6. Females may be viewed from the Greek perspective as hysteric; males as paranoid. This conforms with H.B. Lewis's (1978) assessment of females as depressive-prone and males as schizophrenic-prone. The Hebrew perspective would not see such a split.[8]

Culture and Coital Position: A Closure
Around Distancing and Gender

Some of these themes can be illustrated by a comparison of dominant heterosexual intercourse positions in the Greek and Hebrew cultures. For the noted psychoanalytically oriented anthropologist,

Geza Roheim, the coital position practiced by a people told *all* about them (see Becker 1971, p. 47). This classic psychoanalytic presumpton is, of course, somewhat of an exaggeration. Nevertheless, some writers do perceive differences between the two cultures. A recent study by Marks (1978) argues for two dominant positions represented in the art and literature of ancient Greece. Either the man stands behind a kneeling or bent-over woman, assuming a "rear entry" position, or he "pins" her to the bed in a man-kneeling face-to-face position. Henderson (1975) has suggested that these two positions are reflected in Lysistrata's speech to the Athenian women in Aristophanes' farce of the same name: "Do not play the lioness upon the knife handle [rear entry] nor raise your slippers to the ceiling [pinned]."

Rosenheim (1980) attempts to psychologize the different patterns in Judaism "varying from insistence on the sole legitimacy of the face-to-face male superior position to granting freedom of experimenting [Rosenheim's term] with different modalities of arousal" (p. 257 cf.) Nedarim, 20b; Kallah, 51a; Gittin, 70a; Maimonides, *Mishna Torah*, Laws of Forbidden Intercourse 21:9, Orah Hayim 240), although the male superior postion is still recommended ("he on top, she on bottom").

Figure 7 presents stylized conceptions of these positions. Several points should be noted. First, the "rear entry" position seems to occur far more frequently in ancient Greece than does the "pinned" position (cf. Marks 1978). Second, it is impossible for us to distinguish the "woman reclining" and "woman curled" subtypes of the Judaic "male superior" position. Whichever subtype was employed in the halachic and biblical interest of promoting pregnancy, it is clear that Judaism does not treat the woman as a sexual object. Indeed, the sexual act must be sanctified. In sexual matters the Jewish man must approach his wife tenderly, work very hard to resolve ill feelings, and be very attentive to satisfying her.

The argument at the end of Chapter 4 can thus be tentatively restated. In the Greek positions the woman receives either freedom to move (the "rear entry" position) or eye contact (the "pinned" position) but not both. In the recommended Jewish position, the "male superior" position (whether "woman reclining" or "woman curled"), the woman may receive both eye contact and freedom to move. These positions, if indeed indicative, seem to express in somewhat different form the duality in the Greek culture between attachment (i.e., eye contact) and individuation (i.e., freedom to move) and the integration of the two in Judaism.

Figure 7

A Bidimensional Delineation of Dominant Hellenic

and Hebraic Heterosexual Coital Positions

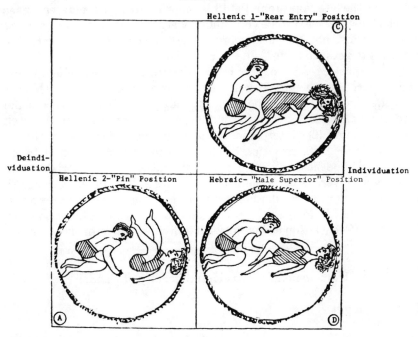

CHAPTER 6

Individuation and Attachment in Greek and Hebrew Thought

In the past decade people have spoken with great confusion about issues of crowding and space, of loneliness and commitment in human relationships. They often seemed unsure of what they wanted from those closest to them, thrashing about in seemingly contradictory ways. As the late Pope John Paul I is reported to have remarked, those in relationships seem to be continuously searching for ways to get out of them; those not in relationships seem to be continuously searching for ways to get into them.

The purpose of this chapter is to compare the way in which union and separation themes emerge in traditional Greek and Hebrew thought. As a working hypothesis, we suggest that (1) interpersonal attachment *decreases* with individuation or differentiation in Greek thought, and (2) interpersonal attachment *increases* with individuation or differentiation in Hebrew thought. We attempt to explore this hypothesis through the examination of two variables: (a) homogeneity versus heterogeneity of gender and (b) fusion versus differentiation of role. Gender homogeneity and role fusion are seen as instances of deindividuation or nondifferentiation; gender heterogeneity and role differentiation as instances of individuation or differentiation.

Homogeneity versus Heterogeneity of Gender

Greek Thought

It is, of course, common knowledge that homosexuality was often a preferred form of social and physical intercourse in Greek thought, whereas it is expressly forbidden in its physical variant in Hebrew thought. We wish to explore here social reasons for this phenomenon and to try to place it within our theoretical model.

There is little doubt that Greek homosexual relationships (male or female) often exhibited a great amount of tenderness and closeness that was typically missing in the heterosexual Greek coupling. Slater

Journal of Psychology and Judaism, Vol. 8(2), Spring/Summer 1984
© *1984 Human Sciences Press*

(1968), among others, has pointed to the pervasiveness of aggressive conflict in the typical Hellenic heterosexual nuclear family.

Greek literature in fact glorifies homosexual love. Plato's *Symposium* and Xenophon's *Symposium* both present men who are much involved in homosexuality. Socrates, who apparently himself had homosexual inclinations, differs from his companions only in arguing that the love of the physical is inferior to the attraction of good personality, whether homosexual or heterosexual. Marriage is not glorified, nor is it ever depicted as preferable to homosexual relationships. The beauty of love of a pretty boy is contrasted favorably with the tribulations of marriage and the degradation of heterosexual intercourse. Socrates, for example, advises Callias to participate more in Athenian government in order to earn the respect of his boy lover.

Greek literature depicts many heterosexual couples at odds, sometimes violently so (see Slater, 1968, p. 37); for example, Zeus and Hera, Agamemnon and Clytemnestra, Jason and Medea, Heracles and Deianeira, and Socrates and Xanthippe. The Greek husband often continued homosexual activities after marriage. Finley (1959) points out that the marital relationship in Homer is more shallow emotionally than relationships between males (pp. 137–138).

In Hellenic thought the marital institution itself is filled with conflict and tension, in Gouldner's (1965) terms a zero-sum game. It is worthy of note that one of the happiest arrangements of the classical period was that of Pericles and the brilliant but foreign-born Aspasia. Because of Aspasia's foreign birth the two could not be legally married in Athens, and Pericles went through many painful years trying in vain to legitimize their children. Such a common-law arrangement held out better hope for a good heterosexual relationship. Pericles went further against the traditional Greek pattern in that he apparently disapproved of homosexuality on moral grounds (Plutarch, Life of Pericles).

Hebrew Thought

The Hebrew Bible, in contrast, explicitly condemns male homosexuality (Leviticus 18:22), and it is, in fact, clear that until modern times homosexuality has never been widespread among Jews. The one exceptional incident recorded in the Hebrew Scripture involves the attempt of some rowdies of the town of Gibeah to have homosexual relations with a traveler. They ultimately gave up unsatisfied their interest in the man and gang-raped his concubine instead. The entire episode was seen as so noxious and repulsive that it provoked a bloody civil war, which resulted in the near annihilation of the tribe of Benjamin, to which Gibeah belonged.[9]

In Judaism male friendships are viewed as highly praiseworthy, but they have no sexual overtones nor are they seen as closer than a heterosexual marriage. The mutual devotion of David and Jonathan is the prime biblical example of a friendship. Both men are married; indeed they are brothers-in-law. The Mishna cites their relationship as an example of love with no ulterior cause (*Avot* 5:7). At the same time, male friendships offer no competition to married life.

The Jewish view sees marriage as a state of great potential joy, of spiritual elevation (*Midrash Shmuel* 48a). Only a married man in most communities may wear the *talit,* and in talmudic Mesopotamia, additionally, the *sudra* (a turban), to indicate his elevated status in the community. There are, of course, marriages that do not succeed, but this is the fault of the immaturity of the individuals—not the institution. Marriage is sacred and preferable to bachelorhood. One's appreciation of a partner's separate personality is enhanced, not degraded, by marital heterosexual intercourse.

The classical literature of the Jews offers a different picture of the marriage situation from that which the Hellenic literature offers its readers. Adam and Eve are created and blessed by God Himself. Marriages, on the whole, seem pleasant and mutually supportive and offer closer levels of intimacy than same-sex relationships.[10] A comparison of Greek and Hebrew views in this regard is presented in Table 2. With regard to the gender issue then, Greek thought seems to view

Table 2

Individuation and Attachment Patterns

in Greek and Hebrew Thought

	Gender		Role Behavior	
	Homogeneity	Heterogeneity	Fusion	Differentiation
Greek Thought	Close	Far	Close	Far
Hebrew Thought	Far	Close	Far	Close

attachment decreasing with diversity. In Hebrew thought, attachment seems to increase with diversity.

Fusion versus Differentiation of Role

In this section we attempt to demonstrate that heterosexual closeness decreases with role differentiation in Greek thought, whereas it increases with role differentiation in Hebrew thought. This analysis requires the disentangling of two commonly confused dimensions: personality characteristics and role behavior. We shall attempt to argue that Greek thought held a polarized view with regard to male and female personalities and valued women who approached masculine role behavior (i.e., who behaved more androgynously with regard to role). In contrast, Hebrew thought tended to have a nonpolarized view with regard to male and female personality but valued women who took on traditional feminine role behavior (i.e., who behaved in a more differentiated role manner). Heterosexual closeness was thus grounded in the level of role similarity in Greek thought (unanchored by any personality compatibility); Hebrew thought anchors heterosexual closeness in the level of personality compatibility (and thus allows role differentiation).

Greek Thought

The Greek mind perceived male and female as highly polarized in personality. Indeed, in perhaps the archetypal story Prometheus is portrayed as autonomous though detached, Pandora as dependent while attached. Yet the feminine personality was portrayed with disdain. As previously mentioned, hysteria was seen by the Greeks as emerging from *hystera*, the Greek term for womb.

On the level of role behavior, the Greeks held up a macho warrior of the Homeric epic type as the ideal for the man. The woman was relegated to the drudgery of the house, a task seen as lacking of honor and not worthy of the husband's respect (see Nietzsche, 1956). The husband and wife were thus set into a competition with each other in which the man would seek to assert himself by subjugating the wife to his macho image, and the wife would avenge herself on the husband by making his family and home life unbearable.

The valued women in Greek thought seemed to take on traditional male roles and behave in a masculine fashion. The type of Athena, Artemis, and the Amazons seeks acceptance by assuming the male function as warrior and huntress.[11] The hetaerae are able to mix with male society by giving up the usual role as house drudge and developing an interest in intellectual and social pursuits. The previously mentioned union of Pericles and Aspasia is an example of a happy relationship involving a woman acting in traditionally male or at least androgynous roles. Aspasia was an educated woman who mixed with the greatest men of her day as an equal. For a man of Pericles' dynamism, marriage to a typical Athenian house drudge would have been miserable. In fact, an earlier marriage had ended in divorce.

Hebrew Thought

The perceptions of male and female personality in Jewish thought do not separate strength and weakness, activity and passivity, and thought and feeling according to gender. Strength, intelligence, activity, and feeling are equally praiseworthy in either. Indeed, the account of Adam and Eve attests to this nonpolarized view of man and woman. Both are striving for attachment and autonomy. The feminine personality is viewed with praise. As mentioned previously, *rahamim*, the Hebrew word for mercy, is from the same root as *rehem*, the Hebrew term for womb, and God Himself is described by this term (*Harahaman*).

At the same time, however, Jewish thought emphasizes the value of role differentiation between man and woman. Although the woman's role was seen as supportive in relation to the man, it is probably safe to say that there is hardly a weak woman in the entire Hebrew Bible. The ideal of the Jewish woman, "the woman of valor" or *eishet chayil* (Prov. 31), gives no hint of passivity. The woman is praised for her abilities in a wide variety of areas—earning money, managing a home, raising children, and caring for the poor. She offers her husband unbegrudging kindness, and he trusts her with a full heart. Her reputation is established by her good works.

Consider now the Jewish view of the male warrior. He does not have a macho personality in the Greek sense. David, for example, is portrayed as a Hebrew shepherd soldier in a single combat against Goliath, a Homeric-style warrior giant (Gordon, p. 1962, 1966).[12] The Philistine challenges the Hebrews in language typical of the warrior's code of honor: "I am the [noble] Philistine and you are slaves to Saul. ... I defy the armies of Israel. Give me a *man* that we may fight together." When Goliath sees a youthful David coming toward him without armor or spear or the usual panoply of the hero, he feels demeaned. "Am I a dog that you come to me with a staff . . ." David's reply characterizes the rejection of war as a heroic endeavor: "You come to me with a sword, and with a spear, and with a shield, but I come to you in the name of the Lord. . . ." (I Samuel 17:1-45) Faith, not military prowess, motivates David. A comparison of the Greek and Hebrew views in this regard is presented in Figure 8.

At the same time role differentiation is quite pronounced in Judaism. Rabbinic law establishes in detail the differences between men and women in regard to the obligation to study Torah. Differences in ritual also are notable. Women are free of most positive commandments that involve an externally imposed time factor. They are much more involved in the particulars of *nida* and *mikva* rituals than are men, functions that emphasize the internal time cycles of their own bodies.

Although the sexes are in one sense quite differentiated, the law also

Figure 8

Gender Stereotypes in Greek and Hebrew Thought

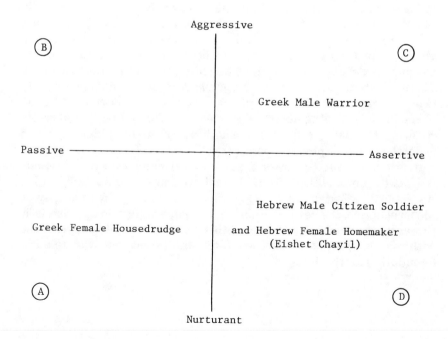

requires the most careful expressions of mutual respect. For example, a tall man with a much shorter wife should not stand over her when they talk but should rather bend over (*Bava Metzia*, 59a). Indeed a man is required to honor his wife above himself (*Yevamot*, 62b). The husband-wife relationship is not inherently competitive. The marital state is viewed as the most productive in terms of mutual support, sexual satisfaction, and individual growth. There is no contradiction between mutuality and individual growth. In fact, the marital state is natural to man. A talmudic dictum holds that if a man reaches the age of twenty and is not married, his bones begin to rot (*Kiddushin*, 29b). If a marriage ends through death or divorce, one should remarry.

It should be noted that in rabbic law marriage is seen as more necessary for the man than for the woman, for the obligation to "be fruitful and multiply" rests solely on the man, not the woman. Also uniquely, sex in marriage is viewed as the man's obligation and the woman's right.

The woman in the Jewish family is not typically unhappy and does not make family life intolerable. We have already mentioned the happy marriages of the biblical patriarchs and matriarchs. Indeed, the traditional mediating role played by the mother between father and son (e.g., Rebecca) tends to soften any inherent sexual rivalry between father and son in an attempt to promote harmony in the Jewish family (see Wellisch, 1954). The major point of differentiation in gender roles is quite clear. The house of study is the man's domain; the woman gladly keeps the light burning in the home and makes it possible for the man to devote himself wholeheartedly to study (*Berakhot*, 17a).[13] These roles are clearly defined by law and are basic to a child's early training. Husband and wife roles are seen as supportive and complementary, not antagonistic or competitive. The woman would rarely challenge the man in scholarship. Similarly, the man could not claim to equal the woman's power of perception.

It is important to stress that one need not be an androgynous Athena to combine the virtues of manly courage with womanly skills. As Table 3 indicates, the Greek definition of androgyny is largely at the level of role; the Jewish definition of compatibility, in contrast is at the level of personality. Because of this, attachment seems to decrease with role differentiation for the Greeks and to increase with role differentiation for the Jews.

Table 3

Gender Personality and Roles in Hebrew and Greek Thought

	Hebrew Thought	Greek Thought
Personality Characteristics	Female Personality Valued: Male and Female Integrated	Female Personality Devalued: Male and Female Polarized
Role Behaviors	Role Differentiation for Women Valued	Role Androgyny for Woman Valued

CHAPTER 7

Narcissus and Jonah: Polarization versus Regression in Greek and Hebrew Individuals

This chapter attempts to explicate a multistage, multilevel approach to individual growth based on the bidimensional distancing analysis presented in the previous two chapters. Cell B is seen as the first stage of development, representing the absence of both *individuation* (i.e., defining one's boundaries) and *attachment* (i.e., taking down one's walls). Cells A, C, A/C, and E are seen as alternate second-stage stops. A represents *attachment without individuation* (i.e., neither walls nor boundaries). C represents *individuation without attachment* (i.e. both walls and boundaries). A/C represents a personality split between A and C. E represents *semi-attachment and semi-individuation* (i.e., moderate walls and moderate boundaries). Cell D is seen as the third stage of development, representing the full presence of *both individuation and attachment.*

Three aspects of this approach should be emphasized. First, there is no route between cell A or cell C and cell D. Cells A and C represent dead ends in terms of moving ahead. The only way out of either of them is through regressing to cell B. Secondly, although one may move ahead from cell B to cell E to cell D (Figure 9a), the movement from A to C occurs through the split cell A/C (Figure 9b). Here a flip-flop occurs between A and C, with no developmental growth to D. Finally, the attainment of cell D (stage 3) at one level opens up the possibility of growth to a more advanced level. However, this more advanced level must be entered at cell B (stage 1)—i.e, the beginning—and the process must be undergone again.

The logic here is that healthy growth involves the graduated and integrated replacement of an interpersonal wall by a self-other boundary. However, taking the wall down prematurely (i.e., before the boundary is strong enough), as in A, or leaving it up too long (i.e., after the boundary has already formed), as in C, leads to the pathological outcomes associated with traditional feminine and masculine socializations. In other words, traditionally stereotyped socializations advance an initially B individual (wall with no boundaries) to either the A position (no walls and no boundaries) or the C position (wall and boundaries). The feminine position (A) is attached at the expense of in-

Journal of Psychology and Judaism, Vol. 8(2), Spring/Summer 1984
© *1984 Human Sciences Press*

dividuation. The masculine position (C) is individuated at the expense of attachment. Only unsatisfactory oscillation between the masculine and feminine positions is possible on the AC axis (reflecting the Jungian yin and yang between the animus and the anima) unless the individual regresses to the B position and moves forward on the BED axis in an integrated manner.

A compelling example emerges regarding the exchange of walls for boundaries in the infant. Prior to birth the fetus is entirely dependent on its mother for nourishment. At the same time the walls of her uterus protect the fetus from the outside environment (cell B). The newborn infant is somewhat less dependent, attached to the breast rather than the umbilical cord, and also is protected somewhat less, by the mother's arms rather than by the uterine walls (cell E). Finally, the infant feeds from a bottle and can do this without the direct bodily protection of the mother. He or she may lie in the crib feeding alone (cell D). This process may well serve as a general metaphor for healthy parenting. Parents need to provide shelter and limits for children not

Figure 9a

Individual Development From the First to the Third Stage

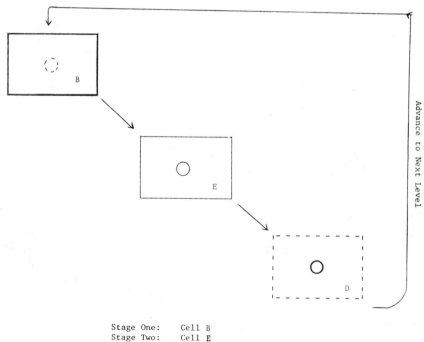

Stage One: Cell B
Stage Two: Cell E
Stage Three: Cell D

yet defined enough to set them for themselves and to lift these limits when they are.

We have attempted to distinguish Greek and Hebrew thought in this regard in the previous two chapters. On the Greek axis no distinction is made between boundaries and walls. Boundaries and walls emerge and disappear simultaneously (i.e., the oscillation between cells C and A). On the Hebrew axis, a very firm distinction emerges between boundaries and walls. Walls disappear as boundaries emerge (the growth from cell B to cell D). What is also crucial here is that a choice between A and C positions is accepted by the Greek mind and rejected by the Hebrew mind, the latter actually preferring a regression to B until coordinated advance is possible. It is important to clarify our usage of the term *regression*. It describes a return to an earlier stage without firm self-other boundaries *but* with protective walls. This concept is very important, as it comprises the focus of the contrast between covenant and narcissism (either in its mirroring or idealizing form).

Figure 9b

Individual Oscillation at the Second Stage

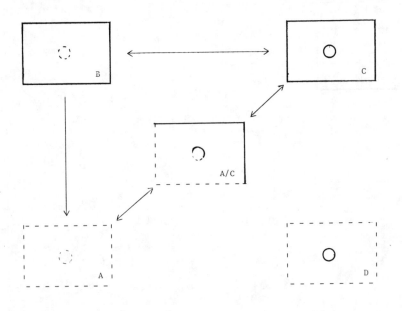

Stage One: Cell B
Stage Two: Cells A, C, A/C
Stage Three: Cell D

Let us attempt to illustrate this theme through the examination of two foundation legends: the myth of Narcissus and the story of Jonah. Slater (1968), for example, sees the myth of Narcissus as prototypical of Greek culture.[14] Likewise, C. Lewis (1972) sees the story of Jonah as a classic Hebrew story in its purposeful simplicity and bluntness.

The Myth of Narcissus

The earliest sources of the myth of Narcissus are long since lost. Our most complete account from antiquity is to be found in the first century Roman poet Ovid's *Metamorphosis* (1955).

The dark river nymph, Liriope, was the first to test his [the seer Tiresias] reliability and truthfulness. She was the nymph whom Cephisus once embraced with his curving stream, imprisoned in his waves, and forcefully ravished. When her time was come, that nymph most fair brought forth a child with whom one could have fallen in love even in his cradle, and she called him Narcissus. When the prophetic seer was asked whether this boy would live to a ripe old age, he replied: 'Yes, if he does not come to know himself.' For a long time this pronouncement seemed to be nothing but empty words: however it was justified by the outcome of events: the strange madness which afflicted the boy and the nature of his death proved its truth.

Cephisus' child had reached his sixteenth year, and could be counted as at once boy and man. Many lads and many girls fell in love with him, but his soft young body housed a pride so unyielding that none of those boys or girls dared to touch him. One day, as he was driving timid deer into his nets, he was seen by that talkative nymph who cannot stay silent when another speaks, but yet has not learned to speak first herself. Her name is Echo, and she always answers back.

Echo still had a body then, she was not just a voice: but although she was always chattering, her power of speech was no different from what it is now. All she could do was to repeat the last words of the many phrases that she heard. Juno had brought this about because often, when she could have caught the nymphs lying with her Jupiter on the mountainside, Echo, knowing well what she did, used to detain the goddess with an endless flow of talk, until the nymphs could flee. When Juno realized what was happening, she said: 'I shall curtail the powers of that tongue which has tricked me: you will have only the briefest possible use of your voice.' And in fact she carried out her threats. Echo still repeats the last words spoken, and gives back the sounds she has heard.

So, when she saw Narcissus wandering through the lonely countryside, Echo fell in love with him, and followed secretly in his steps. The more closely she followed, the nearer was the fire which scorched her: just as sulphur, smeared round the tops of torches, is quickly kindled when a flame is brought near it. How often she wished to make flattering overtures to him, to approach him with tender pleas! But her handicap prevented this, and would not allow her to speak first; she was ready to do what it would allow, to wait for sounds which she might re-echo with her own voice.

The boy, by chance, had wandered away from his faithful band of comrades, and he called out: 'Is there anybody here?' Echo answered: 'Here!' Narcissus stood still in astonishment, looking round in every direction, and cried at the pitch of his voice: 'Come!' As he called, she called in reply. He looked behind him, and when no one appeared, cried again: 'Why are you avoiding me?' But all he heard were his own words echoed back. Still he persisted, deceived by what he took to be another's voice, and said, 'Come here, and let us meet!' Echo answered: 'Let us meet!' Never again would she reply more willingly to any sound. To make good her words she came out of the wood and made to throw her arms round the neck she loved: but he fled from her, crying as he did so, 'Away with these embraces! I would die before I would have you touch me!' Her only answer was: 'I would have you touch me!' Thus scorned, she concealed herself in the woods, hiding her shamed face in the shelter of the leaves, and ever since that day, she dwells in lonely caves. Yet still her love remained firmly rooted in her heart, and was increased by the pain of having been rejected. Her anxious thoughts kept her awake, and made her pitifully thin. She became wrinkled and wasted; all the freshness of her beauty withered into the air. Only her voice and her bones were left, till finally her voice alone remained; for her bones, they say, were turned to stone. Since then, she hides in the woods, and, though never seen on the mountains, is heard there by all: for her voice is the only part of her that still lives.

Narcissus had played with her affections, treating her as he had previously treated other spirits of the waters and the woods, and his male admirers too. Then one of those he had scorned raised up his hands to heaven and prayed: 'May he himself fall in love with another, as we have done with him! May he too be unable to gain his loved one!' Nemesis heard and granted his righteous prayer.

There was a clear pool, with shining silvery waters, where shepherds had never made their way; no goats that pasture on the mountains, no cattle had ever come there. Its peace was undisturbed by bird or beast or falling branches. Around it was a grassy sward, kept ever green by the nearby waters; encircling woods sheltered the spots from the fierce sun, and made it always cool.

Narcissus, wearied with hunting in the heat of day, lay down here: for he was attracted by the beauty of the place, and by the spring. While he sought to quench his thirst, another thirst grew in him, and as he drank, he was enchanted by the beautiful reflection that he saw. He fell in love with an insubstantial hope, mistaking a mere shadow for a real body. Spellbound by his own self, he remained there motionless, with fixed gaze, like a statue carved from Parian marble. As he lay on the bank, he gazed at the twin stars that were his eyes, at his flowing locks, worthy of Bacchus or Apollo, his smooth cheeks, his ivory neck, his lovely face where a rosy flush stained the snowy whiteness of his complexion, admiring all the features for which he was himself admired. Unwittingly, he desired himself, and was himself the object of his own approval, at once seeking and sought, himself kindling the flame with which he burned. How often did he vainly kiss the treacherous pool, how often plunge his arms deep in the waters, as he tried to clasp the neck he saw! But he could not lay hold upon himself. He did not know what he was looking at, but was fired by the sight, and excited by the very illusion that deceived his eyes. Poor foolish boy, why vainly grasp at the fleeting image that eludes you? The thing you are seeing does not exist: only turn aside and you will lose what you love. What you see is but the shadow cast by your reflection; in itself it is nothing. It comes with you, and lasts while you are there; it will go when you go, if go you can.

No thought of food or sleep could draw him from the spot. Stretched on the shady grass, he gazed at the shape that was no true shape with eyes that could never have their fill, and by his own eyes he was undone. Finally he raised himself a little. Holding out his arms to the surrounding woods: 'Oh you woods,' he cried, 'has anyone ever felt a love more cruel? You surely know, for many lovers have found you an ideal haunt for secret meetings. You who have lived so many centuries, do you remember anyone, in all your long years, who has pined away as I do? I am in love, and see my loved one, but that form which I see and love, I cannot reach: so far am I deluded by my love. My distress is all the greater because it is not a mighty ocean that separates us, nor yet highways or mountains, or city walls with close-barred gates. Only a little water keeps us apart. My love himself desires to be embraced: for whenever I lean forward to kiss the clear waters he lifts up his face to mine and strives to reach me. You would think he could be reached—it is such a small thing that hinders our love. Whoever you are, come out to me! Oh boy beyond compare, why do you elude me? Where do you go, when I try to reach you? Certainly it is not my looks or my years which you shun, for I am one of those the nymphs have loved. With friendly looks you proffer me some hope. When I stretch out my arms to you, you stretch yours towards me in return: you laugh when I do, and often I have marked your tears when I was weeping. You answer my signs with nods, and, as far as I can guess from the movement of your lovely lips, reply to me in words that never reach my ears. Alas! I am myself the boy I see. I know it: my own reflection does not deceive me. I am on fire with love for my own self. It is I who kindle the flames which I must endure. What should I do? Woo or be wooed? But what then shall I seek by my wooing? What I desire, I have. My very plenty makes me poor. How I wish I could separate myself from my body! A new prayer this, for a lover, to wish the thing he loves away! Now grief is sapping my strength; little of life remains for me—I am cut off in the flower of my youth. I have no quarrel with death, for in death I shall forget my pain: but I could wish that the object of my love might outlive me: as it is, both of us will perish together, when this one life is destroyed.'

When he had finished speaking, he returned to gazing distractedly at that same face. His tears disturbed the water, so that the pool rippled, and the image grew dim. He saw it disappearing, and cried aloud: 'Where are you fleeing? Cruel creature, stay, do not desert one who loves you! Let me look upon you, if I cannot touch you. Let me, by looking, feed my ill-starred love.' In his grief, he tore away the upper portion of his tunic, and beat his bared breast with hands as white as marble. His breast flushed rosily where he struck it, just as apples often shine red in part, while part gleams whitely, or as grapes, ripening in variegated clusters, are tinged with purple. When Narcissus saw this reflected in the water—for the pool had returned to its former calm—he could bear it no longer. As golden wax melts with gentle heat, as morning frosts are thawed by the warmth of the sun, so he was worn and wasted away with love, and slowly consumed by its hidden fire. His fair complexion with its rosy flush faded away, gone was his youthful strength, and all the beauties which lately charmed his eyes. Nothing remained of that body which Echo once had loved.

The nymph saw what had happened, and although she remembered her own treatment, and was angry at it, still she grieved for him. As often as the unhappy boy sighed 'Alas,' she took up his sigh, and repeated 'Alas!' When he beat his hands against his shoulders she too gave back the same sound of mourning. His last words as he gazed into the familiar waters were: 'Woe is me for the boy I loved in vain!' and the spot re-echoed the same words. When he said his last farewell, 'Farewell!' said Echo too. He laid down his weary head on the green grass, and death closed the eyes which so admired their owner's beauty. Even then, when he was received into the abode of the dead, he kept looking at himself in the waters of the Styx. His sisters, the nymphs of the spring, mourned for him, and cut off their hair in tribute to their brother. The wood nymphs mourned him too, and Echo sang her refrain to their lament.

The pyre, the tossing torches, and the bier, were no being prepared, but his body was nowhere to be found. Instead of his corpse, they discovered a flower with a circle of white petals round a yellow centre.

When this story became known, it brought well-deserved fame to the seer Tiresias. It was told throughout all the cities of Greece, and his reputation was boundless. (Ovid, *Metamorphosis III*, 1.343–511).

The myth of Narcissus has been employed in classic psychoanalytic thinking to refer to an individual who is totally self-absorbed—that is, one who is narcissistic rather than object-invested (cf. Freud, 1914; Hartmann, 1964). For Freud, maturation involves the replacement of narcissism by investment in the object world. Close examination of this myth, however, suggests a somewhat more complicated analysis that is closer, in fact, to Kohut's differentiation between idealizing and mirroring narcissistic configurations. For Kohut (1971), unlike Freud, "narcissism is defined not by the target of the instinctual investment (i.e., whether it is the subject himself or other people) but by the nature or quality of the instinctual charge" (p. 26). Thus, an idealizing configuration whereby one invests his energy in the omnipotent other is seen by Kohut as narcissistic as is the withdrawal of psychic energy inward into the grandiose self (i.e., the mirroring configuration). The intent behind the idealizing configuration is as inherently self-serving ("You are perfect and I am part of you") as is that behind the mirroring configuration ("I am perfect").

The following events in the myth may be highlighted from this perspective.

1. A seer prophesied that Narcissus would live to a ripe old age provided that he never knew himself (Ovid, *Metamorphosis* III, 1 347–349).

2. Although anyone would have fallen in love with him, he heartlessly rejected lovers of both sexes because he had a stubborn pride (hubris) in his own beauty. Among these lovers was Echo, who had no voice of her own and could only reflect back what Narcissus said. Narcissus rejected Echo roughly, saying, "I will die before I would have you touch me" (1. 359–400).

3. One of those Narcissus had scorned, raised his hands to heaven and prayed: "May he himself fall in love with another, as we have done with him! May he too be unable to gain his loved one!"

4. Nemesis, hearing this righteous prayer, caused Narcissus to fall in love with his own reflection in a brook. At first Narcissus tried to embrace and kiss the beautiful boy who confronted him (1. 408–433).

5. Subsequently, he recognized himself and lay gazing at his image for hours. "How I wish I could separate myself from my body!" (1. 463).

6. Grief was destroying him, yet he rejoiced in the knowledge that his other self would remain true to him. Crying "alas" (which Echo repeated), Narcissus pined away unto death (1. 480–495).

These events fit Kohut's analysis of mirroring and idealizing transference quite well. Through the first part of the myth, Narcissus tends to be self-absorbed, treating his lovers as mere extensions or mirrors of himself. This trend becomes accentuated in his relationship with Echo, who becomes a perfect mirror for Narcissus, reflecting back everything Narcissus says. Indeed, Echo has no voice of her own. Narcissus is diagrammed in Figure 10 as a C position—individuated and detached.

Now, however, something happens. A rejected suitor prays that Narcissus himself will experience unrequited love. Nemesis answers this prayer, causing Narcissus, for the first time, to fall hopelessly in love, losing himself in his idealization of the face in the brook. This, of course, represents Kohut's idealizing transference and may be diagrammed as an A position in Figure 10—deindividuated and attached.

Suddenly, however, Narcissus recognizes that the face in the brook is his. It is his double or doppelgänger (see Rank 1971). This reflection becomes simultaneously an ideal and a mirror. He is not self-invested but self-empty, driven to grasp his missing self, which has now been projected into the outside world. He strives to remerge with his now separated double. Such a psychotic juxtaposition rips Narcissus apart. As Ovid expresses it, "How I wish I could separate myself from my body!" Narcissus is now simultaneously at the A/C positions (again see Figure 10). Such a schizoid self-knowledge is unbearable and he resolves the dilemma through suicide, confirming the prophecy of the seer.

The Book of Jonah

Consider, in contrast, the Book of Jonah in the Hebrew Bible.

Chapter 1. Now the word of the Lord came unto Jonah the son of Amittai, saying, Arise, go to Nineveh, that great city, and cry against it; for

Figure 10

Narcissus

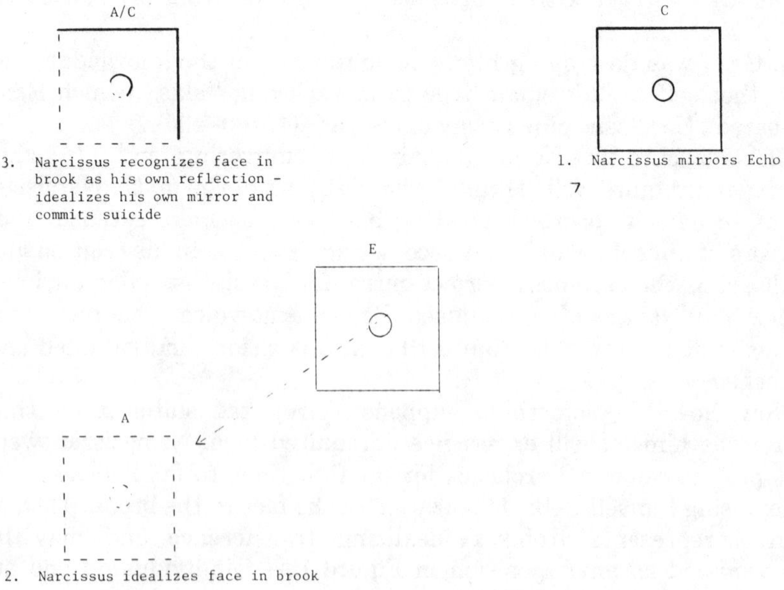

A/C

3. Narcissus recognizes face in
    brook as his own reflection -
    idealizes his own mirror and
    commits suicide

C

1. Narcissus mirrors Echo

7

E

A

2. Narcissus idealizes face in brook

their wickedness is come up before me. But Jonah rose up to flee unto Tarshish from the presence of the Lord, and went down to Joppa; and he found a ship going to Tarshish: so he paid the fare thereof, and went down into it, to go with them unto Tarshish from the presence of the Lord. But the Lord sent out a great wind into the sea, and there was a mighty tempest in the sea, so that the ship was like to be broken. Then the mariners were afraid, and cried every man unto his god, and cast forth the wares that were on the ship into the sea, to lighten it of them. But Jonah was gone down into the sides of the ship; and he lay, and was fast asleep. So the shipmaster came to him, and said unto him, What meanest thou, O sleeper? arise, call upon thy God, if so be that God will think upon us, that we perish not. And they said every one to his fellow, Come, and let us cast lots, that we may know for whose cause this evil is upon us. So they cast lots, and the lot fell upon Jonah. Then said they unto him, Tell us, we pray thee, for whose cause this evil is upon us; What is thine occupation? and whence comest thou? what is thy country? and of what people art thou? And he said unto them, I am a Hebrew; and I fear the Lord, the God of heaven, which hath made the sea and the dry land. Then were the men exceedingly afraid, and said unto him, Why hast thou done this? For the men knew that he fled from the presence of the Lord, because he had told them. Then said they unto him, What shall we do unto thee, that the sea may be calm unto us? for the sea wrought, and was tempestuous. And he said unto them, Take me up, and cast me forth into the sea; so shall the sea be calm unto you: for I know that for my sake this great tempest is upon you. Nevertheless the men rowed hard to bring it to the land; but they could not: for the sea wrought, and was tempestuous against them. Wherefore they cried unto the Lord, and said, We beseech thee, O Lord, we beseech thee, let us not perish for this man's life, and lay not upon us innocent blood: for thou, O Lord, hast done as it pleased thee. So they took up Jonah, and cast him forth into the sea: and the sea ceased from her raging. Then the men feared the Lord exceedingly, and offered a sacrifice unto the Lord, and made vows.

Now the Lord had prepared a great fish to swallow up Jonah. And Jonah was in the belly of the fish three days and three nights.

Chapter 2. Then Jonah prayed unto the Lord his God out of the fish's belly, And said, I cried by reason of mine affliction unto the Lord, and he heard me; out of the belly of hell cried I, and thou heardest my voice. For thou hadst cast me into the deep, in the midst of the seas; and the floods compassed me about: all thy billows and thy waves passed over me. Then I said, I am cast out of thy sight; yet I will look again toward thy holy temple. The waters compassed me about, even to the soul: the depth closed me round about, the weeds were wrapped about my head. I went down to the bottoms of the mountains; the earth with her bars was about me for ever; yet hast thou brought up my life from corruption, O lord my God. When my soul fainted within me I remembered the Lord: and my prayer came in unto thee, into thine holy temple. They that observe lying vanities forsake their own mercy. But I will sacrifice unto thee with the voice of thanksgiving; I will pray that that I have vowed. Salvation is of the Lord. And the Lord spake unto the fish, and it vomited out Jonah upon the dry land.

Chapter 3. And the word of the Lord came unto Jonah the second time, saying, Arise, go unto Nineveh, that great city, and preach unto it the preaching that I bid thee. So Jonah arose, and went unto Nineveh, according to the word of the Lord. Now Nineveh was an exceeding great city of three days' journey. And Jonah began to enter into the city a day's journey, and he cried, and said, Yet forty days, and Nineveh shall be overthrown.

So the people of Nineveh believed God, and proclaimed a fast, and put on sackcloth, from the greatest of them even to the least of them. For word came unto the king of Nineveh, and he arose from his throne, and he laid his robe from him, and covered him with sackcloth, and sat in ashes. And he caused it to be proclaimed and published through Nineveh by the decree of the king and his nobles, saying, Let neither man nor beast, herd nor flock, taste any thing: let them not feed, not drink water: But let man and beast be covered with sackcloth, and cry mightily unto God: yea, let them turn every one from his evil way, and from the violence that is in their hands. Who can tell if God will turn and repent, and turn away from his fierce anger, that we perish not? And God saw their works, that they turned from their evil way; and God repented of the evil, that he had said that he would do unto them; and he did it not.

Chapter 4. But it displeased Jonah exceedingly, and he was very angry. And he prayed unto the Lord, and said, I pray thee, O Lord, was not this my saying, when I was yet in my country? Therefore I fled before unto Tarshish: for I knew that thou art a gracious God, and merciful, slow to anger, and of great kindness, and repentest thee of the evil. Therefore now, O Lord, take, I beseech thee, my life from me; for it is better for me to die than to live.

Then said the Lord, Doest thou well to be angry? So Jonah went out of the city, and sat on the east side of the city, and there made him a booth, and sat under it in the shadow, till he might see what would become of the city. And the Lord God prepared a gourd, and made it to come up over Jonah, that it might be a shadow over his head, to deliver him from his grief. So Jonah was exceeding glad of the gourd. But God prepared a worm when the morning rose the next day, and it smote the gourd that it withered. And it came to pass, when the sun did arise, that God prepared a vehement east wind; and the sun beat upon the head of Jonah, that he fainted, and wished in himself to die, and said, It is better for me to die than to live. And God said to Jonah, Doest thou well to be angry for the gourd? And he said, I do well to be angry, even unto death. Then said the Lord, Thou hast had pity on the gourd, for the which thou hast not laboured, neither madest it grow; which came up in a night, and perished in a night: And should not I spare Nineveh, that great city, wherein are more than sixscore thousand persons that cannot discern between their right hand and their left hand; and also much cattle? (Jonah)

Many writers dismiss Jonah as another "reluctant prophet" or simply a lesser Job (see Lewis, 1972). Others see him as largely motivated by political considerations. One interpretation is that Jonah felt that the continuing existence of Nineveh, capital of the warlike Assyrians, posed a military threat to the Hebrews, who would thus benefit from Nineveh's destruction. Others argue that Jonah worried that if the Ninevites did repent, the Hebrews might look bad by comparison. He flees in the hope that prophetic messages will no longer reach him when he leaves the soil of the Holy Land. In any case Jonah is seen as deliberately working against the will of God in the mistaken view that Jonah's own plans are preferable (cf. Abravanel, Malbim, Gr'a, Radak). Nevertheless, Jonah's decision to flee is puzzling in view of the fact that other prophets openly debated their differences with God; for example, Abraham (Gen: 18), Moses (Exod. 3, 4). Hosea (Pesahim 87b) and Yalkut Shimoni 515) and Jeremiah (Jer. 1). Close examination of the narrative suggests that Jonah is caught in an authentic identity crisis. His regressions to resolve this internal dilemma are made possible by God's covenantal protection. This saves Jonah from the fate of Narcissus. The following events in the narrative may be highlighted from this perspective.

1. Jonah was ordered by God to go to Nineveh to warn it of its wickedness. Jonah attempted to escape God by running away to Tarshish (Jon. 1:1-3).

2. God sent a great wind after him, endangering his ship. When asked his identity by his shipmaster, Jonah admitted to being the cause of the storm. Jonah asked his shipmates to throw him into the sea to spare them. They did so, and he was swallowed by a great fish prepared by God. (1:4-2:1).

3. Jonah prayed to God out of the fish's belly. "I am cast out of thy sight; yet I will look again toward thy holy temple." The Lord spoke to the fish, and it vomited Jonah out upon the dry land (2:3-11).

4. God sent Jonah to Nineveh a second time. This time Jonah went and gave the people of Nineveh God's message. They repented and were saved, but Jonah expressed his anger that they were saved (3:1-4:4).

5. Jonah left the city and sat outside to see what would become of it. God prepared a gourd to shield Jonah from the sun (4:5-6).

6. God then destroyed the gourd. When Jonah mourned the gourd, the Lord said, "Thou hast had pity on the gourd, for which thou hast not labored, neither madest it grow; which came up in night and perished in a night. And should not I spare Nineveh, that great city, wherein there are more than sixscore thousand persons that cannot discern between their right hand and their left hand; and also much cattle" (4:7-11).

Lewis (1972) suggests that Jonah is presented with a terrible dilemma in the beginning of the story. As can he seen in Jonah's later words, Nineveh respresents a symbol of evil to him, and he thinks that it should not be spared through God's mercy. He does not want to be corrupted (absorbed) by Nineveh's wickedness nor does he want to remain aloof from it (abandon it). In Lewis's terms, "he is too God-fearing to defy and too opinionated to submit."

In Figure 11 Jonah is drawn as rejecting both positions C (deindividuated attachment) and A (individuated detachment). Instead, Jonah tries to escape to Tarshish, regressing (1a) in confusion. Jonah confesses to his shipmates that he is responsible for the storm God sent upon them. God saves him from drowning by providing the protective wall of a fish—cell B (deindividuated and detached). Jonah then moves ahead (2a) to position E (semi-individuated and semiattached). This process is initiated by Jonah's prayer from the fish's belly: "I am cast out of thy sight; yet I will look again toward thy holy temple." God responds by removing the protective wall, causing the fish to vomit up Jonah.

When God asks Jonah to go to Nineveh a second time, he goes; but

Figure 11

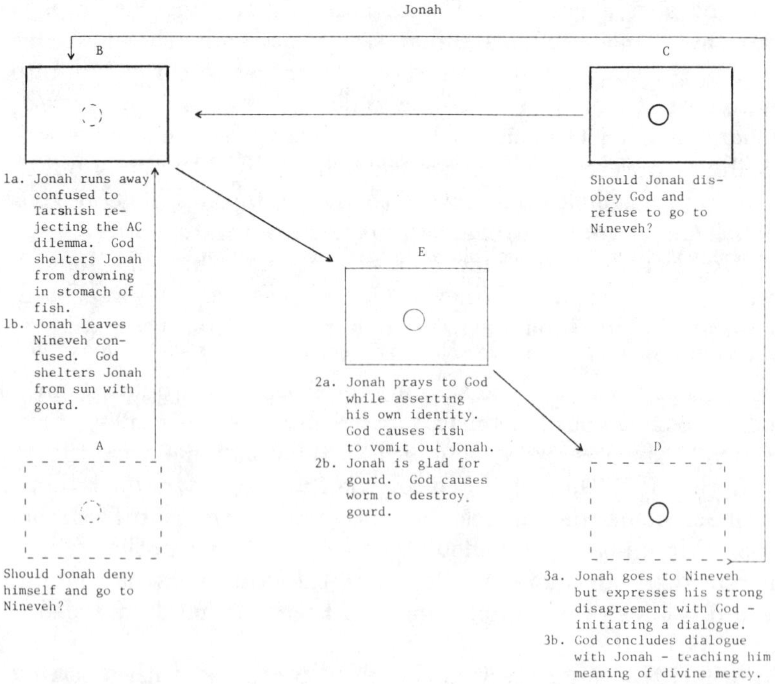

Jonah

B

C

1a. Jonah runs away confused to Tarshish rejecting the AC dilemma. God shelters Jonah from drowning in stomach of fish.
1b. Jonah leaves Nineveh confused. God shelters Jonah from sun with gourd.

Should Jonah disobey God and refuse to go to Nineveh?

E

2a. Jonah prays to God while asserting his own identity. God causes fish to vomit out Jonah.
2b. Jonah is glad for gourd. God causes worm to destroy gourd.

A

Should Jonah deny himself and go to Nineveh?

D

3a. Jonah goes to Nineveh but expresses his strong disagreement with God - initiating a dialogue.
3b. God concludes dialogue with Jonah - teaching him meaning of divine mercy.

this time he stands up to God, expressing his anger that the people of Nineveh are to be saved. This is diagrammed as a move to (3a) position D (individuated attachment). Jonah regresses yet a second time (1b), though at a higher level. This time he sits outside the walls of Nineveh in anger and confusion. God again (as a protective parent would) provides a sheltering wall for Jonah—a gourd to shield him from the sun. Jonah is then moved to cell E (2b). God destroys the gourd with a worm, again removing the protective wall and setting the stage for his subsequent conversation with Jonah, who is now strongly defined enough to hear God's response in the dialogue (3b). God proceeds to instruct Jonah on the value of divine mercy—cell D (i.e., how to remain connected to Nineveh without being corrupted by its wickedness).

Most commentators (e.g., Radak) see Jonah's disappointment in 4:1-3 as motivated by the fear that the Lord in His mercy had pardoned the Ninevites and that the threat to the Hebrews has not been lifted. Bachrach (1967), however, offers an additional point. Jonah, he argues, was convinced that the Ninevites' repentance was superficial and incomplete, and he went to sit outside the city to see if he was right.

Jonah was angry at God for forgiving the Ninevites on what seemed such poor grounds. God then pounds home to Jonah the realization of the magnitude of divine patience and mercy for all mankind. This, of course, requires a strong enough sense of self to overcome one's fear of absorption. It was in order to teach him this lesson that God kept the covenant with Jonah during his confusion and then dispatched him to Nineveh a second time rather than appointing some other prophet.[15]

Greek versus Hebrew Individuals: An Appraisal

Jonah's situation reflects the ups and downs of the covenantal relationship. Even in his nadir at the end of chapter 1 he never completely loses his sense of that special relationship. Closely intertwined with this is the fact that Jonah, although willful, never truly neglects his human responsibilities. He accepts the blame for the storm. Narcissus, in contrast, vacillates between hubris (position C) and nemesis (position A). In an ironic turn of the biblical phrase, Narcissus can love neither his neighbor nor himself. Jonah does not become schizophrenic as does Narcissus (the AC split—A/C). Rather, he twice goes through a temporary regressive process (B) in which God unfolds to him a more realistic perspective on himself and a more useful response to situations (see especially Gr'a). God shelters him in his temporary helplessness as a mother would—first in the fish's belly, then with the gourd. Each of these walls is lifted at the appropriate time. This may well represent the differences between schizophrenia (A/C), narcissistic oscillation or the borderline position (vacillation between A and C), and phase-appropriate withdrawals (B) (cf. Laing and Esterson, 1970).[16] These patterns are summarized in Table 4.

The story of Jonah depicts the Judaic conception of covenant as neither a leap of faith nor a skeptical distrustful bargaining (note the contrast with Shestov's views, Chapter 2). Man does not abdicate his responsibility either by tossing it all into God's lap (i.e., idealizing narcissism) or by entirely rejecting God's claims upon him (i.e., mirroring narcissism). This interpretation is spelled out in the rabbinic understanding of the Jews' acceptance of the Sinaitic covenant "we will do and we will hear" (*Naaseh Venishma*). (See Levovitz, *Daat Chochma Umussar II*, 154–156).

The story of Jonah also may provide a lesson for overcoming the constant-energy model implicit in the myth of Narcissus. For Narcissus energy is invested inward or it is invested outward. When it is pulled in both directions (toward his own reflection), it leads to Narcissus' suicide. Jonah, in contrast, may reject a unipolar distribution of energy, preferring to retreat and reduce energy to both sources until it becomes possible to invest in both of them equally and ultimately, resulting in a mature covenantal dialogue with God. (See Abravanel, Jon. 4:9).

Table 4

Narcissus and Jonah: Individual Growth in Greek and Hebrew Thought

Narcissus			Jonah		
Act	Move	Outcome	Act	Move	Outcome
Narcissus mirrors and abandons Echo	C	Mirroring Narcissism	Jonah refuses to go to Nineveh. Runs away in confusion. God sends fish to save him from drowning.	B_1	Level One Regression
Narcissus idealizes and is absorbed by face in brook.	A	Idealizing Narcissism	Jonah becomes stronger God causes fish to vomit Jonah out on dry land.	E_1	Level One Emergence
Narcissus recognizes face in brook as his own. He idealizes his own mirror.	A/C	Suicide	Jonah goes to Nineveh but later expresses strong disagreement with God.	D_1	Level One Dialogue
			Jonah sits outside Nineveh in confusion. God shields him from the sun with gourd.	B_2	Level Two Regression
			Jonah becomes stronger. God causes worm to eat gourd.	E_2	Level Two Emergence
			God teaches Jonah the message of mercy: to help others without being absorbed by them.	D_2	Level Two Dialogue

CHAPTER 8

Prometheus-Pandora and Adam-Eve: Polarization versus Regression in Greek and Hebrew Couples

In this chapter we attempt to apply the Narcissus-Jonah analysis to couples. The outline of a multi-stage, multi-level approach to couple growth is presented in Figures 12, 13a and 13b. Cell BB is seen as the first stage of couple development. It represents two people, neither truly individuated nor attached to each other. Each is afraid of both abandonment and absorption. As such, they will engage in what we call a *regressed reciprocal relationship,* conflict emerging when each becomes too intimate with the other or too remote ($\leftrightarrows \leftrightarrows$). Each of the parties has strong walls up because the boundaries are not yet developed.

Cells AA, CC, AC, and EE represent alternate second-stage stops. In cell AA, both parties are afraid of abandonment but not absorption (i.e., they are attached but not individuated). Therefore they will

Figure 12

A Bidimensional Distancing Taxonomy of Couple Types

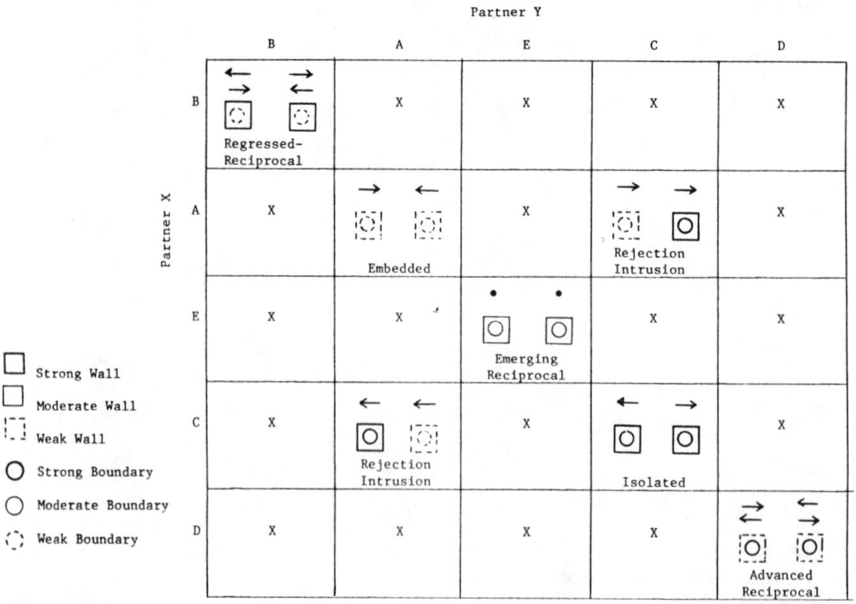

Journal of Psychology and Judaism, Vol. 8(2), Spring/Summer 1984
© *1984 Human Sciences Press*

engage in what Minuchin calls an *enmeshed* or *embedded* relationship, conflict emerging when the two people become too remote from each other (→ ←). Neither party has a wall to protect its lack of boundaries and therefore looks to the omnipotent other to save it from itself (i.e., they are both idealizing narcissists). In cell CC, in contrast, both parties are afraid of absorption but not abandonment (i.e., they are individuated but not attached). They will engage in what Minuchin (1974) calls a *disengaged* or *isolated* relationship, conflict emerging when the parties in the couple become too intimate with each other (← →). Both parties put unnecesary walls up in addition to their overly grandiose sense of self (i.e., they are both mirroring narcissists). Cell AC represents what Jurg Willi (1982) calls a *narcissistic collusion* (p. 76). Partner C is the mirroring narcissist, afraid of entrapment by his partner and looking to substitute the ideal self of the partner. Partner A is the idealizing narcissist, afraid of individual responsibility and abandonment by his partner and looking for a substitute self in the partner (Kohut, 1971). The C partner is so grandiose because the A partner is effusively adoring and vice-versa. In behavioral terms the A partner continually approaches (desires a "we"-ness), and the C continually avoids (wants an "I"-ness). This fits what Napier (1978) has labeled the *rejection-intrusion* relationship, one partner continually wanting more closeness, the other more (→ →)[17] (cf. Feldman 1982a, 418).

Cell EE represents yet another second-stage position, one in which

Figure 13a

Couple Development From the First to the Third Stage

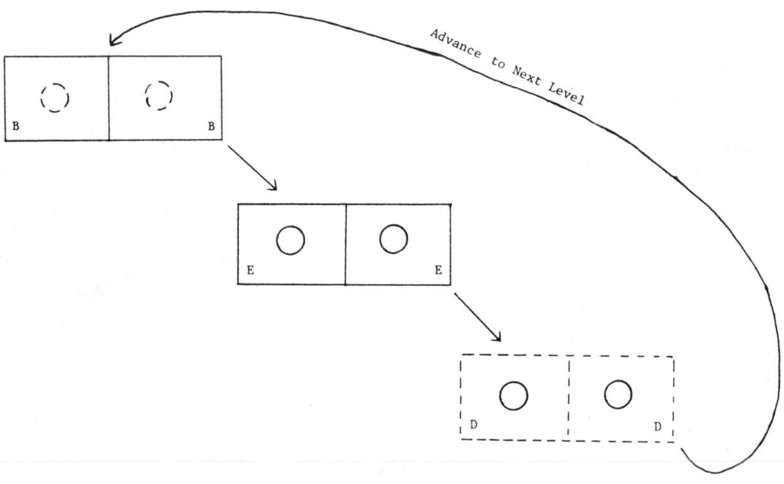

each partner is semi-individuated and semi-attached. Neither partner completely fears abandonment nor absorption, nor has either completely overcome his fears. They are in a half-way position on all fronts and will engage in what appears to be a static relationship, neither partner having too much intimacy or too much space (• •). However, we think that this is the only healthy second-stage position and thus label it as an *emerging reciprocal* position.

Finally, cell DD represents a third-stage couple position. It represents two highly individuated and attached partners, neither afraid of abandonment nor absorption. As such, they will engage in what we call *advanced reciprocal relationships,* coordination occurring between mutual desires for intimacy and space (= =).

What can be seen in Figure 12 is that there is no route between any of the A-C pairings and position DD. They only oscillate among themselves. (AA-AC-CC). The only way out of this box is regression[18] to cell BB and coordinated advance, first to EE and finally to DD.

The logic here is the same as for individuals. Healthy growth for couples as well as for individuals involves the graduated and integrated replacement of an interpersonal wall by a self-other boundary. This is the crux of the entire difference between narcissistic collusion and covenantal development. Taking walls down prematurely or leaving them up too long has the effect of trapping a couple on the narcissistic axis, either in symmetrical (AA or CC) or nar-

Figure 13b

Couple Oscillation at the Second Stage

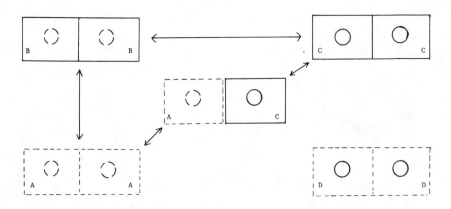

cissistic (AC) collusion (cf. Willi, 1982). The assurance of covenantal protection, in contrast, allows them to regress temporarily to the BB position and move slowly ahead as they become stronger. We now attempt to examine this hypothesis by comparing two Greek and Hebrew couples.

Prometheus and Pandora; Deucalion and Pyrrha

The choice of Prometheus-Pandora requires some justification. Actually, they are not a couple at all. It is Prometheus' brother Epimetheus who is married to Pandora. Yet the leading male and female roles in this story are played by Prometheus and Pandora, although there is no evidence in the myth that they ever met each other. This lack of a "true" original couple may in itself be of the utmost significance to the Greek view of male-female relationships.

The fifth century Sophist, Protagoras, in Plato's dialogue of that name (320c–322d) uses the myth of Prometheus as the basis for an anthropological account of the development of mankind. Because of Epimetheus' foolish unplanned distribution of natural equipment and power to living creatures, the human race was left naked and defenseless. Epimetheus ran out of gifts to give before he got to men. So Prometheus gave mankind fire and the technical arts, stolen from Hephaestus and Athena.

These dynamics portray Epimetheus as a slow-witted stick figure. Despite the marriage of Pandora to Epimetheus, the real dynamic seems, in fact, to exist between Pandora and Prometheus. Consider the following highlighted events (cf. Chapter 4 for the full narrative):

1. Epimetheus distributes natural equipment and power stupidly, giving all to the living creatures but leaving nothing for man.
2. His brother Prometheus steals fire and the mechanical arts for man from the gods.
3. Zeus punishes Prometheus by leading him to a mountain where an eagle tears at his liver.
4. Zeus obtains further revenge by sending a deceitful and seductive woman, Pandora, to Epimetheus.
5. Prometheus warns Epimetheus against becoming entrapped by Pandora.
6. Prometheus is unsuccessful and Epimetheus marries Pandora.
7. Pandora opens Epimetheus' jar, releasing evils into the world.
8. From Pandora comes the race of woman and female kind.

In a sense Epimetheus represents man, with Prometheus and Pandora (and behind her, Zeus) fighting for his soul. Epimetheus fails to carry out the job of achieving autonomy. Prometheus successfully intervenes, stealing fire and the technical arts for man—in short the technical advances that are the basis for human civilization (Plato, *Protagoras*, 320–322d). Prometheus can thus be diagrammed as a C in Figure 14.[19] At the same time Prometheus unsuccessfully warns Epimetheus against becoming entrapped by Pandora (and Zeus). Pandora can be diagrammed as an A, releasing evils such as sickness and old age into the world, forces designed to make man dependent once again.

Epimetheus is thus a passive object in this volatile dance of polarities between Prometheus and Pandora. The dance itself represents an excellent example of the narcissistic collusion described by Willi (1982, p. 76) in which the following contract emerges. Prometheus is ruthless (warning Epimetheus against Pandora) because Pandora is entrapping (undoing Prometheus' hard-won autonomy through opening Epimetheus' jar of evils) and vice versa.[20]

Figure 14

Prometheus and Pandora

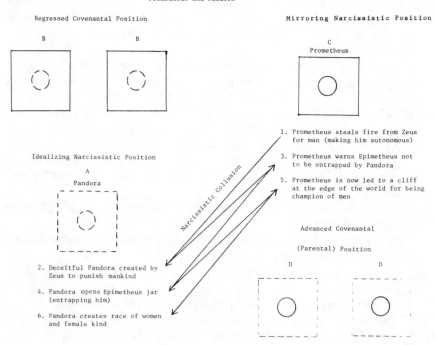

Regressed Covenantal Position

Mirroring Narcissistic Position

B   B

C
Prometheus

Idealizing Narcissistic Position

A

Pandora

Narcissistic Collusion

1. Prometheus steals fire from Zeus for man (making him autonomous)

3. Prometheus warns Epimetheus not to be entrapped by Pandora

5. Prometheus is now led to a cliff at the edge of the world for being champion of men

Advanced Covenantal

(Parental) Position

2. Deceitful Pandora created by Zeus to punish mankind

4. Pandora opens Epimetheus jar (entrapping him)

6. Pandora creates race of women and female kind

D   D

Zeus's acquiescence and even desire for this type of narcissistic male-female relationship is evidenced by his role in the entire affair. First, it is his actions that help create Prometheus' and Pandora's polarized interactional styles. It is, after all, Zeus who withholds fire from man, forcing Prometheus to steal it. It is Zeus who makes Pandora deceitful and sends her to entrap man. Finally, it is Zeus who attempts to maintain the respective narcissistic positions of man and woman by arranging for their separate descent. The race of "woman and female kind" comes from Pandora (position A).

This polarized pattern is further illustrated in the story of Zeus's flood and Deucalion and Pyrrha.

> Prometheus had a son, Deucalion, who was king of the region around Phthia. He married Pyrrha, the daughter of Epimetheus and Pandora, who was the first woman and was made by the gods. Now when Zeus wished to destroy the race of bronze, Deucalion, following Prometheus' advice, built an ark, put in provisions, and entered it with Pyrrha. Zeus caused a heavy rain to fall and submerged the greater part of Greece, with the result that all of mankind was drowned except for a few who fled to nearby high mountains. At that time the mountains of Thessaly were separated, and all the land outside the Isthmus and the Peloponnese was flooded. Deucalion was carried through the sea in the ark for nine days and nine nights and then came to rest on Parnassus. When the rain stopped he emerged from the ark and sacrificed to Zeus as the god of Escape. Zeus sent Hermes to him and granted him a wish. He asked for mankind to come into being. On Zeus' instructions he had Deucalion and Pyrrha pick up stones and throw them over their heads. The stones he threw became men, the ones Pyrrha threw, women. From this comes the word "people" (laoi), metaphorically from "stone" (laas). (Apollodorus, 1976, 1.7-2.)

Ovid chooses to focus on Deucalion and Pyrrha, good and decent people (one of the poet's few happy couples), who are lonely for human company. They pray to Themis (not to Zeus, as in Apollodorus), and eventually puzzle out the goddess's instructions to toss their mother's bones over their shoulders (their "mother" is Earth, her "bones" are stones that re-people the wet and empty world). (Ovid, Metamorphosis 1. 1-125-449).

The following events in the above narratives may be highlighted for our purposes:

1. Deucalion is the son of Prometheus. Pyrrha is the daughter of Pandora (and Epimetheus).
2. Zeus sends a flood to destroy the race of Bronze without warning Deucalion and Pyrrha.

3. Prometheus warns Deucalion and advises him how to build an ark.
4. Deucalion and Pyrrha are saved by the ark during the flood and are described as a happy couple.
5. After the flood Deucalion and Pyrrha emerge from the ark and ask the gods (either Zeus or Themis depending on the account) for renewal of the human race.
6. Zeus responds by re-creating men from Deucalion and women from Pyrrha (rather than from their sexual union).

Figure 15 attempts to place this story in schematic form. In the beginning of the narrative Pyrrha and Deucalion seem to fall into the A-C narcissistic collusion displayed by their respective parents, Pandora and Prometheus. Zeus sent a flood because of a personal affront. His narcissistic attempts to drown them seems to drive them into a symmetrical A-A collusion. Prometheus' intervention seems to push them into the opposite polarity, a C-C collusion against Zeus. They escape the flood by becoming estranged from Zeus. Miraculously, their time together on the ark seems to tilt them off their narcissistic collusion, seemingly establishing the beginning of a covenantal relationship (position B-B). Ovid describes them as a happy couple. Rather than allow this relationship to mature, however, Zeus quickly

Figure 15

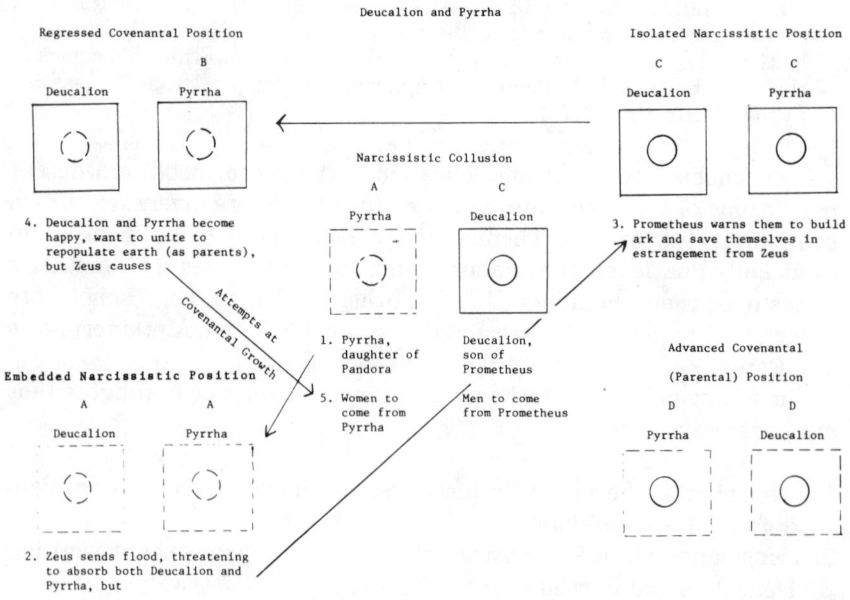

Deucalion and Pyrrha

repolarizes it, causing women to come from Pyrrha and men from Deucalion, re-establishing the original A-C narcissistic collusion.

Adam and Eve; Noah and His Wife

The choice of Adam and Eve requires no justification, of course. They are the first biblical couple. Their story has been presented in Chapter 4 and is highlighted below.

1. God creates Eve, a helpmate for Adam, from his rib (Gen. 2:21–24).
2. God commands Adam (and Eve) not to eat of the tree of knowledge lest they die (2:16–17).
3. The serpent entraps Eve to eat of this tree; Eve entraps Adam (3:1–6).
4. Adam and Eve hide from God, denying their act (3:8).
5. Adam blames Eve; Eve blames the serpent (3:12–13).
6. God clothes them in their confusion (3:20).
7. Instead of killing them, he exiles them from Eden (3:22–24).
8. In exile they come to know the pain and toil of earning a livelihood and raising children (4:1).

Adam and Eve are in an initial dilemma. Like Jonah, they are too God-fearing to disregard totally His commandment (position C) and too opinionated to submit (position A). Yet they fall into exactly this A-C pattern with each other. The woman is entrapped by the serpent to eat of the tree. She in turn entraps Adam to do likewise. Adam relatiates by blaming Eve; she, in turn, blames the serpent. Beneath Eve's entrapment of Adam lies a fear of abandonment, of taking the responsibility and consequences alone for her act. Thus, Figure 16 portrays her as initally in the A position. Beneath Adam's blaming, in contrast, lies a fear of absorption, which appears in his effort to place the entire responsibility on Eve and avoid any share himself. He is initially in the C position. This pattern, of course, represents the same narcissistic collusion as that displayed by Prometheus and Pandora, Adam blaming because Eve is entrapping. However, the biblical God, unlike Zeus, will have none of it.

Indeed, some commentators argue that the reason for God's exile of Adam and Eve is exactly his disapproval of this narcissistic pattern. For example, a well-known midrash (Gen. Rabbah, 19:12) states that the main reason that the man and woman were driven from the garden was that each attempted to blame someone else for their sin (also see

Rashi, Gen. 3:12). Similarly, Eve's entrapment of Adam can be seen as an attempt on her part to avoid solitary death. "She [Eve] came to him and said: Do you think that I will die and another Eve will be created for you? Do you think that if I die you will survive me?" (Gen. Rabbah, 20:8).

Despite his anger at their narcissistic pattern, God's covenant with them remains unimpaired. He does not kill them but provides them with clothing (a wall) to protect them in their exile and confusion (a weak boundary). This, of course, allows Adam and Eve to retreat back to position B-B (the regressed reciprocal position). They then begin to develop their marital relationship, learning to live with the labor and pain of life and parentage (position E-E). They ultimately demonstrate a still higher level of development by bearing a third son, Seth, after the murder of Abel and the banishment of Cain (position D-D).

Put another way, Adam and Eve are initially in their own narcissistic collusion. The mirroring narcissist (Adam) is afraid of absorption, and the idealizing narcissist (Eve) is afraid of abandonment. Adam is ruthless (blames Eve for eating of the tree) because Eve attempts to entrap him (seduces Adam to eat of the tree). However, they tilt off the narcissistic contract to one based on covenant. Adam and

Figure 16

Adam and Eve

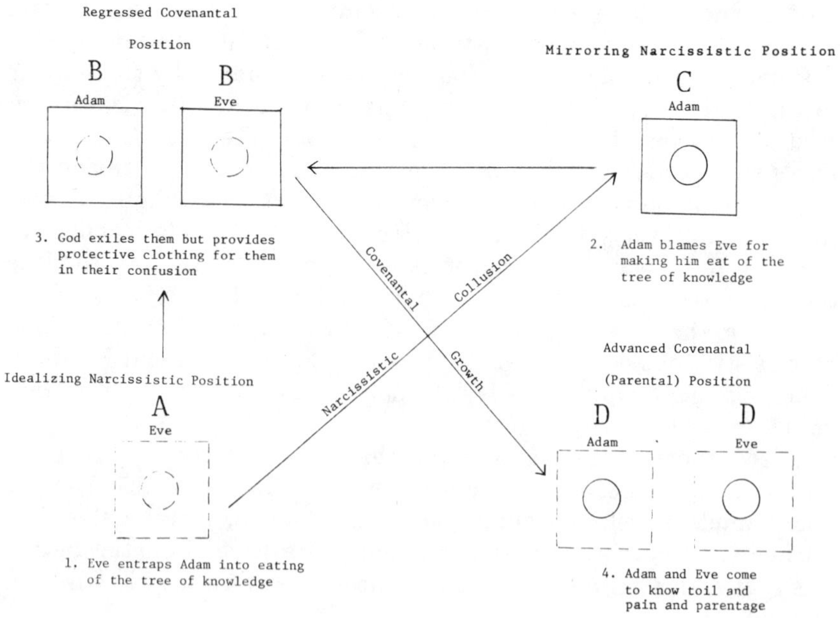

Regressed Covenantal
      Position   Mirroring Narcissistic Position

   B   B   C
Adam   Eve   Adam

3. God exiles them but provides   2. Adam blames Eve for
   protective clothing for them   making him eat of the
   in their confusion   tree of knowledge

Idealizing Narcissistic Position   Advanced Covenantal
                                                (Parental) Position
       A   D   D
      Eve   Adam   Eve

   1. Eve entraps Adam into eating   4. Adam and Eve come
      of the tree of knowledge   to know toil and
                                                 pain and parentage

Eve hide in confusion (no boundaries) and are clothed by God (protective walls). This regression is a necessary preliminary to a coordinated advance and joint parentage.

The same covenantal pattern emerges in the narrative of Noah and his wife. First, the descent of Noah (and his wife) from Adam and Eve is asserted (Gen. 5:1–32). God then warns Noah of the impending flood and makes arrangements for his safety.

The following events in the story of Noah may be highlighted:

1. Noah (and his wife) are descendants of Adam and Eve (Gen. 5:1–32)
2. God sends a flood to destroy man (6:5–17), but
3. God warns Noah and instructs him how to build an ark and to save two or more of each creature, male and female (6:13–22).
4. After the flood Noah and his wife and all the creatures, male and female, repopulate the earth according to God's design (8:15–19, 9:1).
5. God places a rainbow in the heavens as a sign of the covenant with man that there will not be another flood (9:12–17).

Figure 17

Noah and his Wife

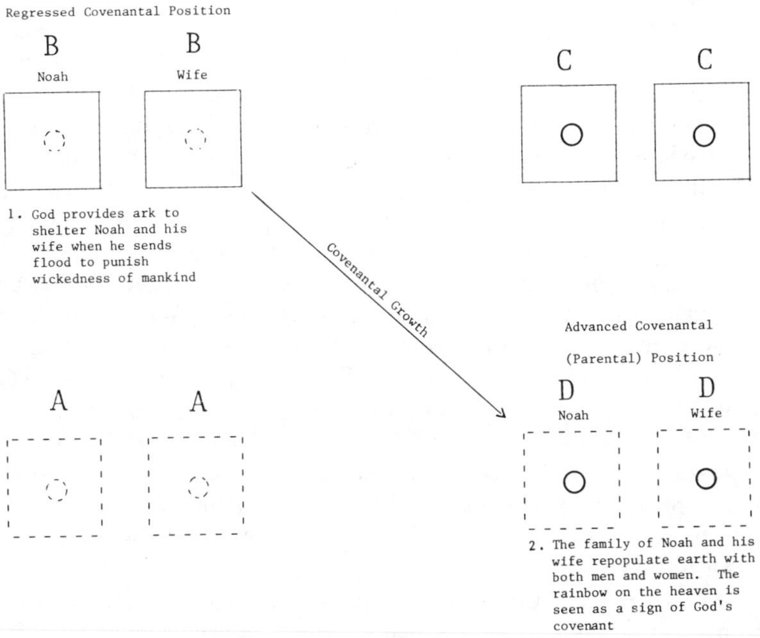

Regressed Covenantal Position

B   B
Noah   Wife

1. God provides ark to shelter Noah and his wife when he sends flood to punish wickedness of mankind

Covenantal Growth

C   C

A   A

Advanced Covenantal

(Parental) Position

D   D
Noah   Wife

2. The family of Noah and his wife repopulate earth with both men and women. The rainbow on the heaven is seen as a sign of God's covenant

Figure 17 attempts to place this story in schematic form. God sends the flood because of mankind's wickedness. However, God, unlike the narcissistic Zeus, does not try to destroy Noah and his wife but provides a covenantal shelter, the ark, to protect them from the flood. This may be diagrammed as a temporary regression on the part of Noah and his wife to the B-B (regressed reciprocal) position. However, God is providing the plan for them to reemerge into a parental D-D (advanced reciprocal) position. New people (both men and women) have come from the union of Noah and his wife. The rainbow in the heavens represents the sign of the covenant even in the face of human sinfulness. [21]

Greek versus Hebrew Couples: An Appraisal

Diametrically opposing techniques emerge in the Greek and Hebrew couple dynamics examined in this chapter. The Greek couples fall into an A-C narcissistic collusion and are kept there by the narcissistic Zeus (A/C). Acquiescence to him (Pandora) or revolt against him (Prometheus), no matter how noble, remains on this narcissistic AC axis. The biblical God (D), in contrast, provides the Hebrew couples with the opportunity for a safe covenantal regression (BB) to allow them to escape their narcissistic collusion and ultimately arrive at an advanced covenantal parental position (DD).

For example, Zeus not only indirectly creates the context whereby Prometheus must steal fire from him (C position) and Pandora is sent to entrap man (A position) but actively intervenes to block the happy couple, Deucalion and Pyrrha, from achieving joint parental status (DD position). In this latter case Zeus calls for separate male and female parentage, bringing forth men from Deucalion (C position) and women from Pyrrha (A position). The biblical God, on the other hand, not only creates a covenantal protection for Noah and his wife (BB), providing the blueprint for the ark and not forcing them to estrange themselves from him to save themselves (as does Zeus in the case of Deucalion and Pyrrha), but also actively interrupts the emerging narcissistic collusion between Adam and Eve. In this case the biblical God enables Adam and Eve to regress off the blaming-entrapping axis.

Zeus and the biblical God can be contrasted as marital therapists. Zeus pushes the couple into narcissistic polarization and collusion (and separate parentage), actively blocking any attempts at covenantal regression and ultimate joint parentage. In contrast, the biblical God moves a couple into a regressed covenantal position making it possible for them to grow into ultimate joint parentage. He actively blocks any attempts at narcissistic collusion and separate parentage (see Table 5).

Table 5a

Couple Growth in Greek and Hebrew Thought

Greek Couples

Prometheus			Pandora		
Act	Move	Outcome	Act	Move	Outcome
Prometheus steals fire from Zeus	C	Mirroring Narcissism	Pandora made deceitful to entrap man	A	Idealizing Narcissism
Prometheus warns Epimetheus against entrapment by Pandora	C	Mirroring Narcissism	Pandora opens Epimetheus' jar of evils	A	Idealizing Narcissism
Prometheus nailed to cliff at edge of world for being benefactor of man	C	Mirroring Narcissism	Race of women come from Pandora	A	Idealizing Narcissism

Deucalion			Pyrrha		
Act	Move	Outcome	Act	Move	Outcome
Son of Prometheus	C	Mirroring Narcissism	Daughter of Pandora	A	Idealizing Narcissism
----- Zeus sends flood to destroy Deucalion and Pyrrha -----					
	A	Idealizing Narcissism		A	Idealizing Narcissism
----- Prometheus provides ark to save Deucalion and Pyrrha in estrangement from Zeus -----					
	C	Mirroring Narcissism		C	Mirroring Narcissism
----- Deucalion and Pyrrha become happy -----					
	B	Regressed Covenantal		B	Regressed Covenantal
----- But Zeus intervenes -----					
Deucalion produces men	C	Mirroring Narcissism	Pyrrha produces women	A	Idealizing Narcissism

Table 5b

Couple Growth in Greek and Hebrew Thought

Hebrew Couples

Adam				Eve	
Act	Move	Outcome	Act	Move	Outcome
Adam blames Eve for eating of the apple	C	Mirroring Narcissism	Eve entraps Adam to eat of the apple	A	Idealizing Narcissism
-----					
God intervenes to exile Adam and Eve but provides protective clothing for them -----					
	B	Regressed Covenantal		B	Regressed Covenantal
----- Adam and Eve come to know toil and pain ----- and take on initial parental function					
	E	Emerging Covenantal		E	Emerging Covenantal
----- Adam and Eve bear Seth after the murder of Abel and the banishment of Cain					
	D	Advanced Covenantal		D	Advanced Covenantal

Noah				Noah's Wife	
Act	Move	Outcome	Act	Move	Outcome
----- Noah and wife, descendants of Adam and Eve -----					
	D	Advanced Covenantal		D	Advanced Covenantal
----- God sends flood but provides ark to save Noah and his wife -----					
	B	Regressed Covenantal		B	Regressed Covenantal
----- Noah and his wife emerge from ark together -----					
	E	Emerging Covenantal		E	Emerging Covenantal
----- The family of Noah and his wife repopulate the earth -----					
	D	Advanced Covenantal		D	Advanced Covenantal

CHAPTER 9

Oedipus and Isaac: Sons in Greek and Hebrew Families

Let us now examine the position of the son in Greek versus Hebrew families. We begin by viewing the nature of the father-son relationship through a comparison of the archetypal stories of Laius and Oedipus versus Abraham and Isaac. We focus here on the role of covenant in general, and covenantal circumcision (*berit hamilah*) in particular, in the Hebrew family and its neutralizing of the son's fear of castration and the father's fear of displacement, apparent in the Greek family. Second, we attempt to differentiate the roles of the mothers in these two types of families, commenting briefly on the respective roles of Jocasta and Sarah in these stories and comparing more fully the stories of Rhea and Zeus and Medea and her sons versus Rebecca and Jacob and Esau. We focus here on the role of nurturer-mediator in the Hebrew family in contrast to that of seductress or murderess apparent in the Greek family.

The Father-Son Relationship: The Oedipus Complex versus the Akedah Motif

Laius and Oedipus and the Greek Father-Son Relationship

The classic myth employed by psychoanalysis to understand the father-son relationship (and indirectly the mother-son relationship) is that of Oedipus, who, as we know, slew his father Laius and married his mother Jocasta. The story of Oedipus may be summarized as follows:

> King Laius of Thebes was warned by an oracle that there was danger to his throne and life if his son, new-born, should reach man's estate. He, therefore, committed the child to a herdsman with orders for its destruction. The herdsman, after piercing the infant's feet gave him to a fellow-shepherd, who carried him to King Polybus of Corinth and his queen, by whom he was adopted and called Oedipus, or Swollen-foot.
>
> Many years afterward, Oedipus, learning from an oracle that he was destined to be the death of his father, left the realm of his reputed sire, Polybus. It happened, however, that Laius was then driving to Delphi,

accompanied only by one attendant. In a narrow road he met Oedipus. A quarrel broke out, and Oedipus slew both Laius and his attendant.

Shortly after this event, Oedipus saved Thebes from the Sphinx, a monster, part woman, part lion, and part eagle, who had been devouring all who could not guess her riddle, "What animal is it that in the morning goes on four feet, at noon on two, and in the evening upon three?" Oedipus correctly replied, "Man, who in childhood creeps on hands and knees, in manhood walks erect, and in old age goes with the aid of a staff."

In gratitude for their deliverance, the Thebans made Oedipus their king, giving him in marriage their queen, Jocasta. He, ignorant of his parentage, had already become the slayer of his father; in marrying the queen he became the husband of his mother. (From Gayley 1893, 261–264)

The Freudian Oedipus complex is taken from this myth and reflects the ambivalent desire of the son to displace his father and possess his mother. It is neutralized by the father's threat of castration, causing the son to give up his mother as a sexual object and identify with the father. This resolution occurs during the phallic stage of development and is the basis of the introjection of the superego (Freud, 1923a, 1923b, 1924).

The term *Oedipus complex* is somewhat of a misnomer. In the ancient myth Oedipus does not merely feel a subconscious urge to kill his father and marry his mother. He actually commits the crimes, albeit because of mistaken identity. What is particularly striking, however, is the behavior of Laius, Oedipus' father. Laius is informed by an oracle that he will bear a son who will one day slay him. He therefore refrains from intercourse with his wife Jocasta except on one occasion when he is thoroughly inebriated. From that one liaison, Oedipus is conceived. Fearing the oracle's prediction, Laius cruelly orders the exposure of his own son on a mountaintop to die. It is only by chance that Oedipus is saved by a shepherd. This myth typifies the underlying conflict in the Greek family between father and son, the mutual fears of destruction by the other.

The lack of an active role by Jocasta is also interesting. The myth indicates no protest on her part either to the lack of physical relationship with her husband or to the piercing and exposure of her son. She seems unable to move toward developing a better family relationship.

It is also worth stressing the role of the Sphinx in this story. She is the personification of all-devouring woman (body of a lion, head of a woman). Her riddle of human development and mortality (four feet in the morning, two feet at noon, and three feet in the evening) is also compelling. Failure to recognize this terrible secret leads to destruction. Oedipus, however, does correctly recognize this secret—yet he is ultimately destroyed through marriage to his mother, Jocasta. It is a tragic irony of this story that accepting this notion of human development and aging leads the Greeks to rejection of generational differentiation (he is given his mother to marry). This illustrates the no-win aspects of the Greek narcissistic culture (see Gutmann, 1980, for a criticism of this "loss perspective" on aging).

This Oedipus myth can be seen as rooted in Freud's larger conception of primitive social organizations and father-son hostilities as expressed in his classic work, *Totem and Taboo* (1913). In primeval times men lived in small hordes, each under the domination of a strong male. All females were his property, the wives and daughters in his own hordes as well as those stolen from other hordes. If the sons excited the father's jealousy, they were killed or castrated or driven out.

Freud suggests that this kind of social organization was altered by a banding together of the driven-out sons, who collectively overcame and murdered the father and ate of his body. This cannibalistic act becomes comprehensible as an attempt by the sons to assume their own identification with the father by displacing him and then incorporating a part of him. [22]

This analysis helps pinpoint the fear of both parties in the father-son relationship. The son is afraid of castration, the father of displacement. Freud suggests that an implicit social contract emerged in time *after* the original killing with the aim of avoiding further conflict. Each of the victorious sons renounced the ideal of gaining for himself the position of father, of possessing his mother or sister. With this, the *taboo* of incest and the law requiring exogamy (and the taboo against eating a *totem*) came into being. In his postulation of the Oedipus complex and its resolution, Freud suggests that the son's fear of castration overpowers his desire to displace the father *before* rather than *after* the murder. Attendant to this resolution is the *taboo* against sexual relations with the mother.

The above analysis suggests more a battle of *manas* (the father's *threat of castration* neutralizing the son's *threat of displacement*) than any true resolution of the dynamics underlying these threats and fears. Whatever the universality of this pattern, there is little doubt that it is common in Greek thought. Indeed Greek father-son myths abound with instances of castration and incorporation.

The world of the gods began with Uranus who was created by Gaea, the Earth. Gaea not only was his mother but also his wife. They founded a family of Titans. It was a tragic feature of Greek mythology that Uranus, the primordial father, violently hated and persecuted his children. Cronos, the youngest son of Uranus, with the help of his mother Gaea, rose against his father, castrating and dethroning him. Cronos in turn swallowed his own children as soon as they were born to avoid being supplanted by them as he was warned by an oracle; however, Zeus, his youngest son, survived, overpowering Cronos with the help of Rhea, his mother, and becoming king. Zeus in turn devoured his wife with the embryo in her womb. Other examples of child incorporation are the stories of Tantalus, Atreus, and Thyestes.

Abraham and Isaac and the Hebrew Father-Son relationship

Contrast the pivotal father-son story in the Hebrew Bible —Abraham's binding of Isaac. This story is known in Hebrew literature under the name of the Akedah. The story is related in the first nineteen verses of the twenty-second chapter of Genesis.

And it came to pass after these things, that God did tempt Abraham, and said unto him, Abraham: and he said, Behold, here I am.

And he said, Take now thy son, thine only son Isaac, whom thou lovest, and get thee into the land of Moriah; and offer him there for a burnt offering upon one of the mountains which I will tell thee of.

And Abraham rose up early in the morning, and saddled his ass, and took two of his young men with him, and Isaac his son, and clave the wood for the burnt offering, and rose up, and went unto the place of which God had told him.

Then on the third day Abraham lifted up his eyes, and saw the place afar off.

And Abraham said unto his young men, Abide ye here with the ass; and I and the lad will go yonder and worship, and come again to you.

And Abraham took the wood of the burnt offering, and laid it upon Isaac his son; and he took the fire in his hand, and a knife; and they went both of them together.

And Isaac spake unto Abraham his father, and said, My father: and he said, Here am I, my son. And he said, Behold the fire and the wood: but where is the lamb for a burnt offering?

And Abraham said, My son, God will provide himself a lamb for a burnt offering: so they went both of them together.

And they came to the place which God had told him of; and Abraham built an altar there, and laid the wood in order, and bound Isaac his son, and laid him on the altar upon the wood.

And Abraham stretched forth his hand, and took the knife to slay his son.

And the angel of the Lord called unto him out of heaven, and said, Abraham, Abraham: and he said, Here am I.

And he said, Lay not thine hand upon the lad, neither do thou any thing unto him: for now I know that thou fearest God, seeing thou hast not withheld thy son, thine only son from me.

And Abraham lifted up his eyes, and looked, and behold behind him a

ram caught in a thicket by his horns: and Abraham went and took the
ram, and offered him up for a burnt offering in the stead of his son.

And Abraham called the name of that place Jehovah-jireh: as it is said
to this day, In the mount of the Lord it shall be seen.

And the angel of the Lord called unto Abraham out of heaven the
second time.

And said, by myself have I sworn, saith the Lord, for because thou
hast done this thing, and hast not withheld thy son, thine only son:

That in blessing I will bless thee, and in multiplying I will multiply
thy seed as the stars of the heaven, and as the sand which is upon the
sea shore; and thy seed shall possess the gate of his enemies;

And in thy seed shall all the nations of the earth be blessed; because
thou hast obeyed my voice.

So Abraham returned unto his young men, and they rose up and went
together to Beer-sheba; and Abraham dwelt at Beer-sheba.

In his work *Isaac and Oedipus* Erich Wellisch (1954) maintains that
the Akedah story provides an unambivalent resolution of the father-
son relationship unavailable in the story of Oedipus. Wellisch suggests
that the moral relationship of parents to their children can be considered in three main stages.

The first and most primitive stage is characterized by intense
aggression and possessiveness of the parents. The aggression is particularly severe in the father and directed mainly to his sons and in the
first place to his firstborn son. In early societies it not infrequently
culminated in infanticide.

The second stage is caused by a reaction of guilt about aggressive and
possessive tendencies and especially about committed infanticide. It
results in a compromise solution between the opposing tendencies of the
wish to possess the child completely or even to kill him and the desire
not to do so (i.e., Freud's Oedipus Complex). . . .

These mental sufferings can only be overcome when the third stage of
moral development of the parent-child relationships is reached. It con-
sists in the entire or almost entire abandonment of possessive,
aggressive and especially infanticidal tendencies and their replacement
by a covenant of love and affection between parent and child. . . .

The Hebrew Bible contains many stories on this subject but none of
them is so important as the story of the binding of Isaac by
Abraham—the Akedah. In the Akedah experience, the third stage of
moral development of the parent-child relationship is reached in a com-
pleteness matched by no other psychological experience. (pp. 3–4).

Wellisch, then, is postulating that the Akedah experience produces
"instinct modification" in the attitudes of parents toward children (at
least fathers toward sons) and vice versa. His argument involves an
extended concept of the superego.

The resolution of the Oedipus Complex is brought about by the emergence of the superego. Its main sources are the introjection of parental and other images and secondary narcissism, and its main effects are moralization, moral masochism and instinct transformation. According to our interpretation of the Akedah motif, the image of man's divine calling is introjected in addition to the images of the parents. The introjected call of God contains an altruistic aim and therefore love for this ego-ideal decreases narcissistic love and increases object-love. (p. 114)

The postulation of a covenantal "divine calling" introject is quite interesting. Nevertheless, Wellisch does not specify the mechanisms by which such introjection comes about. Wellisch's views in this regard have received severe criticism in psychoanalytic circles. Even someone as sympathetic to Wellisch as Theodore Reik views Wellisch's claim for a "modification of instincts" in the *Akedah* experience as a psychological impossibility (Reik 1961, p. 225).[23]

Wellisch's claim does receive more concrete support, however, from closer examination of Freud's previously presented reasoning with regard to primitive fathers and sons. The son threatens displacement of the father, taking over his power as symbolized by possession of the mother.[24] The father threatens castration in response. The resolution of the Oedipus complex may be seen as a neutralization of these two forces, the threat of displacement balanced by the threat of castration. Nevertheless, the problem underlying these threats remains as do the respective fears. What is this problem? In our minds it is the lack of a full psychological acceptance of the right of a human being to develop, whereby a son may inherit the position of his father and is encouraged to surpass him.

This, of course, is exactly the problem that the biblical covenant addresses. The father is not owner of the son as with the Roman *patria potestas,* nor does he hold the power of infant exposure. The relationship of father and son is seen in terms of fulfillment of the covenant. The child honors the father and the mother as an aspect of obedience to God, not of personal obligation to the parent. The urge of father and son to destroy each other is superseded by the obligation of both to the covenant. The father's great joy is to be able to instruct his son in the covenant and to see him carrying it on. One of the most significant themes in the rabbinic literature is the command to the father to teach his son thoroughly (Deut. 6:7; *Kiddushin* 30a). The father's identity is not threatened by the son. Indeed, he wants to see his son develop and surpass him

It is particularly significant psychologically that the covenant is in part symbolized by physical circumcision, performed on Jewish male children at 8 days of age.[25] The Hebrew Bible thus seems to offer an unambivalent resolution for both the father's fear of displacement and the son's fear of castration (and murder). The father willingly passes down the covenant, making displacement by the son unnecesary.[26] The son in turn becomes increasingly aware that the father could have castrated him but chose not to, instead offering a sanctified noninjurious circumcision as the very symbol of his (the father's) love and assent to the son's right to succession.[27] This pattern results in an overall increased security, making attacks on the other unnecesary.

The outcome of this analysis is, of course, that suggested by Wellisch—a covenantal relationship typified by a compassionate love and passing down of a tradition from father to son as in the families of Abraham, Isaac, and Jacob. Emphasis shifts from competition between father and son to a united effort toward fulfilling the covenant, symbolized by circumcision and involving a total dedication to the acceptance and carrying out of the divine will.

The role of the mother in the covenantal family also is fundamentally different. She too is part of the covenant and plays a major role in its continuance. She has no need to defend or avenge herself by pitting her husband and sons against each other (Gen. 28:5; Hirsch, Gen. 27:42). In the Genesis narratives Sarah arranges for the removal of Ishmael and Hagar when their presence appears to threaten Isaac's attachment to the covenant, and God Himself supports her. All this is in stark contrast to the passivity of Jocasta in the Oedipus account and indeed to the entire tone of the story.

The Mother-Son Relationship: Seductress-Murderess versus Nurturer-Mediator

We have briefly compared the behavior of Jocasta and Sarah in the above stories. Jocasta behaves in a passive manner throughout the account, Sarah in an active and vigorous manner. Jocasta unknowingly marries her son, the seemingly unwitting murderer of her husband. Sarah is deeply devoted as both mother and wife, clearly differentiating the two roles. A fuller distinction emerges from the comparison of the Greek accounts of Rhea and Zeus and of Medea and her sons with the Hebrew account of Rebecca and Jacob and Esau.

Rhea and Zeus, Medea and Her Sons,
and the Greek Mother-Son Relationship

Examination of the role of the mother in the Greek family presents
another link in the chain of interlocking hostility and conflict. Indeed,
it was Philip Slater's (1968) studies of the families in Greek mythology
that led him to focus on the mother-son relationship as potentially
more destructive than that between father and son. The mother's low
self-esteem intensifies her already existent (and realistic) fear of being
abandoned. She responds to her miseries by using the sons to hurt the
husband, thus venting her rage on those who she feels keep her in her
wretched state. By hurting her children despite her maternal instincts,
she also expresses her guilt and self-hatred. The mother thus acts as a
force for disharmony and conflict within the family, typically
triangulating with the son against the father—in the role of either seductress or murderess. This accounts for the oral-narcissistic dilemma.
The mother threatens to seduce or murder the son; the son in turn
rejects her and may well keep his distance from all women (often
becoming homosexual).

Consider first the account of Rhea's collusion with her son Zeus in
his vengeance against Cronus, his father:

> Cronus married his sister Rhea, to whom the oak is sacred. But it was
> prophesied by Mother Earth, and by his dying father Uranus, that one
> of his own sons would dethrone him. Every year, therefore, he
> swallowed the children whom Rhea bore him: first Hestia, then Demeter
> and Hera, then Hades, then Poseidon.
>
> Rhea was enraged. She bore Zeus, her third son, at dead of night on
> Mount Lycaeum in Arcadia, where no creature casts a shadow and
> having bathed him in the River Neda, gave him to Mother Earth; by
> whom he was carried to Lyctos in Crete, and hidden in the cave of Dicte
> on the Aegean Hill.
>
> Around the infant Zeus's golden cradle, which was hung upon a tree
> (so that Cronus might find him neither in heaven, nor on earth, nor in
> the sea) stood the armed Curetes, Rhea's sons. They clashed their spears
> against their shields, and shouted to drown the noise of his wailing, lest
> Cronus might hear it from far off. For Rhea had wrapped a stone in
> swaddling clothes, which she gave to Cronus on Mount Thaumasium in
> Arcadia; he swallowed it, believing that he was swallowing the infant
> Zeus. Nevertheless, Cronus got wind of what had happened and pursued
> Zeus, who transformed himself into a serpent and his nurses into bears:
> hence the constellations of the Serpent and the Bears.
>
> Zeus grew to manhood among the shepherds of Ida, occupying

another cave; then sought out Metis the Titaness, who lived beside the Ocean stream. On her advice he visited his mother Rhea, and asked to be made Cronus's cup-bearer. Rhea readily assisted him in his task of vengeance; she provided the emetic potion, which Metis had told him to mix with Cronus's honeyed drink. Cronus, having drunk deep, vomited up first the stone, and then Zeus's elder brothers and sisters. They sprang out unhurt and, in gratitude, asked him to lead them in a war against the Titans, who chose the gigantic Atlas as their leader; for Cronus was now past his prime. . . .

Cronus, and all the defeated Titans, except Atlas, were banished to a British island in the farthest west (or, some say, confined in Tartarus), and guarded there by the Hundred-handed Ones; they never troubled Hellas again. Atlas, as their war-leader, was awarded an exemplary punishment, being ordered to carry the sky on his shoulders; but the Titanesses were spared, for the sake of Metis and Rhea. Zeus himself set up at Delphi the stone which Cronus had disgorged. It is still there, constantly anointed with oil, and strands of unwoven wool are offered upon it. (Graves 1955, pp. 39–41)

Rhea here is portrayed quite differently from Jocasta in the Oedipus account. She is not a passive victim of unwitting patricide. Rather she is an active seductress, instigating or at least colluding in Zeus's move to displace Cronus. This is perhaps one of the two most vivid examples of a Greek woman's hatred for her husband and her willingness to use her sons to gain revenge.

Consider the second example in more detail—that of Medea, who goes so far as to murder her sons to wreak vengeance upon her husband, Jason. The wretched state of woman and the brutality to which it drives her are expressed in Euripides' magnificent drama *Medea*. The legend of Medea's aid to Jason and the Argonauts in their quest for the golden fleece is among the best known of the ancient Hellenic tales and it also forms the subject of the third-century epic poem the *Argonautica*, by Apollonius of Rhodes.

The action in Euripides' *Medea* begins when Jason rejects Medea some years later to marry a wealthy princess of Corinth. Medea reacts with bitter rage against Jason, emphasizing her suffering: "She [Medea] lies without food and gives herself up to suffering, wasting every moment of the day in fear" (pp. 24-26). She plots a terrible revenge, the murder of the new bride and of Medea's own two sons with Jason. As the plot develops, Medea expresses her feelings. She resents the misery that comes with being a woman, and she resents both Jason and her sons: "I hate you, children of a hateful mother, I curse you and your father" (1. 112-114). A man's role is so much pleasanter. She despises her role as a woman.

A man when he's tired of company in his home
Goes out of the house and puts an end to his boredom.
And turns to a friend or companion of his own age.
But we are forced to keep our eyes on one alone.
What they say of us is that we have a peaceful time.
living at home, while they do the fighting in war.
How wrong they are. I would very much rather stand three
times in the front of battle than bear one child. (1. 244–251)

Medea cannot bear the thought of being rejected and abandoned by Jason or of being mocked by her enemies. Jason criticizes Medea for being illogical and impractical. Jason's misogyny and disdain for women are clear. Men are truly superior.

It would have been better far for men
To have got their children in some other way and women,
Not to have existed. Then life would have been good. (1. 573–575)

Medea hates Jason's disdain for her sex but essentially agrees with it. The woman's role disgusts her. Medea will not be a weak, feeble-spirited stay-at-home. Rather she plots to wound Jason deeply.

Medea sends Jason's bride a beautiful white dress and a golden crown as wedding gifts. However, they have been treated with poison so that they burn the princess to an agonizing death when she puts them on. Medea then completes her revenge with the murder of the two boys. In the final scene, Medea appears above the house in a chariot drawn by flying dragons. The bodies of her sons are with her. Jason pleads to be allowed to bury them. Medea torments him and rebukes him cruelly.

No, it was not to be that you should scorn my love,
And pleasantly live your life through, laughing at me (1. 1354–55)
I too, as I had to, have taken hold of your heart. (1. 1360)

Medea is motivated, largely by the feeling that Jason was abandoning her. If she could not be with him any longer in marriage, she would still be united with him—"take hold of your heart"—by her horrible deed. She has at last succeeded in gaining the full attention of her husband. Jason may now hate her, but he can no longer scorn her as weak, powerless, and irrational. Medea has proved herself cleverer and more macho than any warrior. She has punished Jason for abandoning her, and at the same time she has repaid her sons for making her a mother and contributing to her abasement.

One cannot call Medea's perception of her situation entirely erroneous. Like Greek women in general she was despised and demeaned by men and often subjected to a very real threat of rejection and abandonment or ill-treatment. What is horrible here is Medea's solution, so self-destructive as well as so frighteningly inhuman to others. It tells much of the deep rage and hostility inherent in the typical role and position of the Hellenic woman, to which she feels she can respond most effectively by destroying the entire family. [28]

The wife in the Greek family is in constant conflict with her husband and uses the sons to hurt him. She may do this by seducing them to displace her husband (like Rhea) or by murdering them (like Medea). The royal couple of the gods, Zeus and Hera, may represent the prime example of this pattern. Hera, bitterly hostile to Zeus, constantly plots the destruction of his numerous bastards. She herself, according to some accounts, bore him no children. The passive role of Jocasta in the Oedipus myth may represent a paler reflection of this deeply hostile pattern on the part of the Greek mother-wife.

Rebecca and Jacob and Esau and the Hebrew Mother-Son Relationship

Such an attitude as that described above—of a wife seducing her son to displace her husband or murdering her son to deprive her husband of an heir—is foreign to the Hebrew family. Indeed, it is unthinkable within a covenantal conception of family.

The woman's status in the family is much honored. She feels less need to compete with her husband and sons. Rather than encourage and exploit the primitive impulse to rivalry between fathers and sons (the Oedipal conflict), she helps promote a sense of harmony between them. Rather than evoke oral incorporative fears in the son through the threat of either seduction or murder, she helps guide the son to manhood as a potential heir of the covenant. Although her role is different from her husband's, it is no less integral. She is truly an *eishet chayil* (a woman of valor).

Rabbinic literature stresses the significance of the woman's support of the Torah study of her husband and sons (*Berakhot* 17a; *Ketubot* 62b), and numerous stories are related like that of the mother of Rabbi Joshua (ca 50–125 CE), who would bring Joshua while still in the cradle to the house of study, so that he would grow accustomed early to the sound of study of the Torah. The rabbis of the Talmud also showed a great respect to their mothers. When Rabbi Joseph heard the footsteps of his mother approaching his house, he would hasten to meet her saying, "Let me rise to meet the Divine Presence" (*Kiddushin* 31b).

A classic example of the Jewish mother is Rebecca. Abraham's servant is sent to Haran to find a suitable wife for Isaac. He tests the women of Haran by asking them for a drink of water from the well. Rebecca is the first to respond to his request and also volunteers to draw water for ten camels, thirsty from their long journey. By this act of kindness and lively intelligence, she proves herself a fit wife for Isaac. (Gen. 24:12–20; see also Abravanel Gen. 24:12)

During her marriage to Isaac and particularly in the incident of the passing down of the blessing. Rebecca proves her kindness, ability, and courage as a wife and mother. Isaac is now an elderly man, dim of sight, who lives a very retiring life. He is drawn toward the vigorous Esau, who posseses a type of earthy physical strength, a wildness, that Isaac himself lacked (Hirsch, Gen. 25;28). Apparently realizing that Jacob is the fitter of his two sons in spiritual matters, he decides to bestow his blessing of material wealth and power on Esau, who will likely need it more than Jacob. Rebecca learns of Isaac's intention and feels that he is mistaken. Jacob will be the follower of Abraham's covenant and will need the support of material well-being, too. Rather than confront Isaac directly, she plans a mummery that will obtain the material blessing for Jacob without bruising Isaac's feelings. When Jacob hesitates, Rebecca assures him that she is the mother and is assuming full responsibility for the plan (Gen. 27:13). The plan succeeds and Jacob receives the assurance of material well-being, "dew of the heavens and the fats of the land and much corn and wine" (Gen. 27:28–29).

Rebecca bears no hatred to Esau, even through the hard times that follow. However, she sees more realistically than Isaac the threat to the continuity of the covenant if Esau and not Jacob should receive the blessing. When Rebecca hears of Esau's fury and his threats to murder Jacob, she again acts in a manner that saves Jacob's life and sets up the basis for the ultimate restoration of harmony to the family. She protects both her sons, whom she still loves (Gen. 27:43, 28:5; she is still "mother of Jacob and Esau") and again avoids hurting Isaac. Without informing Isaac of Esau's threats and without filling his ears with "I told you so's" about Isaac's mistaken view of Esau, she suggests to Isaac that it would be suitable for Jacob to go to Haran to find a wife, as indeed Eliezer had done for Isaac himself. Isaac agrees without even realizing the full danger in the situation and gives Jacob the spiritual blessing that he had planned for him all along (Gen. 28:3).

"And give thee the blessing of Abraham to thee and to thy seed with thee" (Gen. 28:4). Jacob now has both the spiritual blessing and material assurance of carrying on the covenant. Family harmony is not shattered, and when Jacob returns to Canaan years later, he and Esau are reconciled.

Rebecca's role as a mediator in the Hebrew family leads first to the successful passing down of the covenant and second to the restoration of family harmony. Throughout, she avoids heightening any father-son rivalry; indeed, she does her best to defuse it. Thus, the third stage of mother-son relationships is reached, overcoming the Rhea-Medea complex in a way not available in the Greek attitude toward life. [29]

CHAPTER 10

Electra and Ruth: Daughters in Greek and Hebrew Families

In this chapter we propose to examine the position of the daughter in Greek versus Hebrew families. We begin by examining the nature of the mother-daughter relationship through a comparison of the archetypal stories of Clytemnestra and Electra versus Naomi and Ruth. We focus here on the role of covenant in general and covenantal purification in particular in the Hebrew family in neutralizing the daughter's shame regarding her own womanhood (especially menstruation), and the mother's expectation of abandonment by the daughter apparent in the Greek family.[30] Second, we attempt to differentiate the role of the father in these two types of families, through a comparison of the stories of Agamemnon and Iphigenia versus those of Jephthah and his daughter and Amram and Miriam. We focus here on the role of protector in the Hebrew family in contrast to the exposer-abandoner apparent in the Greek family.

The Mother-Daughter Relationship: The Electra Complex versus the Ruth Motif

Clytemnestra and Electra and the Greek Mother-Daughter Relationship

The classic myth employed by psychoanalysis to understand the mother-daughter relationship (and indirectly the father-daughter relationship) is that of Electra. Electra, as we know, participated in the slaying of her mother Clytemnestra in retaliation for Clytemnestra's slaying of her husband and Electra's father, Agamemnon.

Basing his play on the myths, Euripides depicts Electra as waiting for years, completely obsessed by her plans for the return of her brother Orestes and their revenge on Clytemnestra, in order to honor "her conquering father" (*Electra* 1.188). Nurtured by both mother and father to see herself as a woman and debased, Electra is hostile both toward men and toward her mother, as well as toward her own lowly role. She is married to a farmer of good family, "one of nature's gentlemen" (1.262). Yet Electra treats him badly and boasts to strangers

Journal of Psychology and Judaism, Vol. 8(2), Spring/Summer 1984
© 1984 Human Sciences Press

that she is still a virgin (1.255). Seeking to entice Clytemnestra into
Electra's house where she can be easily murdered, Electra sends to tell
Clytemnestra that she has just now given birth. When Clytemnestra
arrives, Electra lets out long-built-up hostility in a lengthy speech,
primarily accusing her mother of betraying Agamemnon with her
lover Aegisthus.

> You, long before your daughter Iphigenia came near sacrifice
> the very hour your husband marched away from home,
> were setting your brown curls by the bronze mirror's light.
> Now any woman who works on her beauty when her man
> is gone from home indicts herself as being a whore.
> She has no decent cause to show her painted face
> outside the door unless she wants to look for trouble.
> Of all Greek women, you were the only one I know
> to hug yourself with pleasure when Troy's fortunes rose,
> but when they sank, to cloud your face in sympathy.
> You needed Agamemnon never to come again.
> And yet life gave you every claim to be wise and fine
> You had a husband scarcely feebler than Aegisthus
> whom Greece herself had chosen as her King and captain;
> and when your sister Helen did the things she did,
> that was your time to capture glory,
> for black evil is outlined clearest
> to our sight by the blaze of virtue.

Clytemnestra's response to Electra is not without insight as to the
preference of the daughter for her father over her mother.

> My child, from birth you always have adored your father.
> This is part of life. Some children always love the male,
> some turn more closely to their mother than him. (1. 1102)

Electra's reaction to the subsequent murder of Clytemnestra further
displays her essential feeling of debasement as a woman.

> O weep for me, where am I now? What dance, what wedding may I come
> to? What man will take me bride to his bed. (1.1198–1200)

Euripides introduces Castor and Pollux as a deus ex machina to
resolve the play. They tell the other characters that their premises for
the murder were wholly erroneous. The gods had not required the
matricide; the oracle had been false. Euripides is very pointedly
challenging the entire Greek thought pattern about families. The one
character in the play whom Euripides admires is the farmer who lives

by common sense nurtured in the wisdom of experience and who seems sensitive to the needs of others. Electra, Orestes, and the others are bound by patterns of family and social relationships that bring misery and ruin to those who follow them.

The Electra complex (as termed by Jung) is taken from this myth and reflects the ambivalent desire of the daughter to abandon her mother and marry her father. It is neutralized through the daughter's giving up of her father as a sexual object and coming to identify with her mother. As the basis for this identification is not punitive (as in the Oedipus complex), it may be accomplished through the introjection of an ego idea.[31] However, in the Freudian scheme the daughter does not rest easy because of the remaining penis envy on her part with regard to her father. What we suggest as one dynamic in this process is a shame of menstruation elicited in the daughter by the mother as a means of neutralizing the mother's own fear of abandonment. Penis envy may be a result rather than a cause of this process.[32]

The term *Electra complex* is somewhat of a misnomer in regard to this analysis. Electra does not threaten to abandon her mother Clytemnestra; rather she conspires with her brother Orestes to murder her. Further, Electra does not do this, strictly speaking, to possess her father, Agamemnon, but in vengeance for his earlier murder at the hands of Clytemnestra and her lover. The murder was at least partly in retaliation for Agamemnon's earlier sacrifice of Electra's sister Iphigenia and his violence toward Clytemnestra's family. In many ways the story of Iphigenia better represents some of these themes (i.e., Iphigenia may have more of an Electra complex than Electra herself). However, we shall discuss this in the context of father-daughter relationships.

The Electra myth can be seen to be rooted in the more general role of the woman in the Greek society. Although the basic relationship between mother and daughter may be potentially the closest of all familial dyadic relationships in a sex-segregated society such as ancient Greece (cf. Slater, 1968, p. 29), it is tainted by the lack of genuine self-esteem available to woman in that society.

Woman in the Greek mind is seen as the mysterious other closely associated with the capricious laws of nature. This "otherness" is stated clearly in the Pandora myth. Pandora is created out of clay; *from her is the race of woman and female kind.* This alienation of the woman is perhaps most clearly expressed in the taboo quality of her menstrual blood—it is unclean. Such taboos lead to envy on her part of the male (cf. Stephens, 1962) and a willingness on the part of the daughter to abandon the mother and to look to her father as a ticket to entrance into civilized society. We postulate that the Greek mother's only defense in this regard is to lower her daughter's self-esteem by eliciting even further shame in the latter's menstrual condition, to make it too risky for the daughter fully to abandon the mother lest she herself wind up totally alone—without her mother *and* without her father.

This, however, obviously does not represent any real solution to the problem. The daughter's low self-esteem still pushes her to abandon her mother and possess her father. Her mother dissuades her from doing this only through evoking a further diminution in her self-esteem achieved by heightening the daughter's shame regarding menstruation. Any attachment between Greek mother and daughter is thus permeated with a symbiotic quality.

Naomi and Ruth and the Hebrew Mother-Daughter Relationship

A significantly different sort of mother-daughter relationship appears in the covenantal Hebrew family. Emphasis shifts from competition between mother and daughter to a united effort toward fulfilling the covenant. The father is not owner of the daughter as with the Roman *patria potestas,* nor does he have the power of child exposure. Rather he becomes involved in the process of child care as a fulfillment of the covenant (cf. Bakan 1979). The child honors the father and the mother as an aspect of obedience to God, not of personal obligation to the parent.

Woman, in the Hebrew mind, is man's partner in civilized society. This partnership is stated clearly in the Eve narrative. Eve is of Adam's flesh and bone; *she is the mother of all living things.* A woman's partnership status is illustrated by the laws of *nidah* (contrary to the claim of many feminists). She enters a ritual bath (*mikva*) and is transformed from the status of unclean to clean. The essential law of *nidah,* put simply, is that a woman ceases sexual contact with her husband at the onset of her menstrual period. Seven days after her period she may immerse herself in the *mikva,* after which full sexual contact between husband and wife may be resumed (Blumenkrantz, 1969; Tendler, 1982). The sexuality of the woman is thus accepted as part of civilized society and she need not be ashamed of her menstrual emission. We again refer to the midrashic interpretation of Numbers, 23:9—that one cannot number the *mitzvot* that Israel fulfills with the seed of sexual intercourse. Semen and menstrual blood are sacred parts of God's creation.

The societal acceptance of the laws of ritual purity influence and confer a status even on a young girl who is not yet married and on a woman who never marries (and who therefore have no need to purify themselves after each menstrual period). Ritual purification represents a tangible symbol of the woman's role in society and thus dampens any fear of abandonment that the young girl might have. She anticipates her own entrance to civilized society and thus need not attempt to abandon her mother and possess her father to achieve security. Likewise, the mother need not evoke shame of menstruation on the part of the daughter. The daughter is not an object to be dispensed with but a person in her own right. [33]

Consider the classic relationship between mother (actually mother-in-law) and daughter in the Hebrew Bible: the love between Naomi and Ruth. After both their husbands die, Ruth refuses to abandon Naomi.

> And Ruth said, Entreat me not to leave thee, or to return from following after thee: for whither thou goest, I will go; and where thou lodgest, I will lodge: thy people shall by my people, and thy God my God:
> Where thou diest, will I die, and there will I be buried: the Lord do so to me, and more also, if ought but death part thee and me.
> When she saw that she was steadfastly minded to go with her, then she left off speaking unto her. (Ruth, 1:7-1:16)

Ruth meets Boaz, a kinsman of Naomi's late husband, who is greatly moved by Ruth's treatment of Naomi (Ruth, 2:11-14). Later Naomi instructs Ruth on how to win Boaz.

> Then Naomi her mother in law said unto her, My daughter, shall I not seek rest for thee, that it may be well with thee?
> And now is not Boaz of our kindred, with whose maidens thou wast? Behold, he winnoweth barley to night in the threshing-floor.
> Wash thyself therefore, and anoint thee, and put thy raiment upon thee, and get thee down to the floor: but make not thyself known unto the man, until he shall have done eating and drinking.
> And it shall be, when he lieth down, that thou shalt mark the place where he shall lie, and thou shalt go in, and uncover his feet, and lay thee down; and he will tell thee what thou shalt do.
> And she said unto her, All that thou sayest unto me I will do.
> And she went down unto the floor, and did according to all that her mother in law bade her. (Ruth 3:1-6)

Finally, Boaz decides to marry Ruth; Naomi becomes nurse to their son, and is even described by the neightbor ladies as the child's mother.

So Boaz, took Ruth, and she was his wife: and when he went in unto her, the Lord gave her conception, and she bare a son.

And the women said unto Naomi, Blessed be the Lord, which hath not left thee this day without a kinsman, that his name may be famous in Israel.

And he shall be unto thee a restorer of thy life, and a nourisher of thine old age: for thy daughter in law, which loveth thee, which is better to thee than seven sons, hath borne him.

And Naomi took the child, and laid it in her bosom, and became nurse unto it.

And the women her neighbours gave it a name, saying. There is a son born to Naomi; and they called his name, Obed: he is the father of Jesse, the father of David. (Ruth 4:13–22)

What comes across clearly in this story is the absence of any desire on the part of Ruth to abandon Naomi in order to marry. Indeed, her loyalty to Naomi is exemplary. Naomi, in turn, does her best to enhance Ruth's self-esteem and instructs her how to approach her kinsman Boaz. After Ruth and Boaz do marry, Naomi is included in their happiness, becoming nurse to their son Obed, who was the father of Jesse, the father of David. The shame-of-menstruation/fear-of-abandonment dilemma implicit in the Greek mother-daughter relationship (and indirectly in the Electra dilemma) is resolved in the Ruth motif through the covenantal transformation of that relationship into "teacher" and "student"—covenantal purification (*nidah*) making the "rawness" of the Hebrew woman civilized. That this relationship should emerge between mother-in-law and daughter-in-law makes it even more powerful. This represents the third stage of mother-daughter relationships akin to that postulated by Wellisch (1954) for father-son relationships.

The Father-Daughter Relationship:
Exposer-Abandoner versus Protector

We have briefly discussed the behavior of Agamemnon and Boaz in the narratives above: Agamemnon shows violence to Clytemnestra's family; Boaz is very kind to Ruth's family. A fuller distinction emerges from the comparison of specific father-daughter accounts: the Greek accounts of Agamemnon and Iphigenia with the Hebrew accounts of Jephthah and his daughter and of Amram and Miriam.

Agamemnon and Iphigenia and the Greek
Father-Daughter Relationship

Examination of the role of the father-daughter relationship in the Greek family presents another link of interlocking hostility and conflict within the nuclear family. The father carries uncertain feelings about his own manhood into the relationship and transmits ambivalent signals to his daughter. First, he demands that she idealize him as a male; second, he treats her as an object of degradation. If she does not idealize him, she is threatened with rejection and abandonment (exposure). At the same time she is so debased that she is worthy of nothing other than rejection and abandonment. Both signals are apparent in Agamemnon's attitude toward Iphigenia. Agamemnon gathered the Greek fleet at Aulis to sail against Troy. However, a seer announced that Artemis was angry and would not send favorable winds. To gain her favor it would be necessary to sacrifice a young maiden; the seer recommends Iphigenia. After some indecision Agamemnon agrees. He sends for Iphigenia to come to the camp on the pretext that she is to marry Achilles, all the while intending to sacrifice her. Agamemnon wastes no feeling of affection on his daughter. She is merely an object that will be destroyed so that Agamemnon can maintain his position as head of the Greek army. Iphigenia, still unaware of her impending doom, desperately needs her father's acceptance, and her playing up to Agamemnon shows both her need for him and the fact that she awards him victory over Clytemnestra in the parents' rivalry for the daughter's loyalty.

> O Mother, don't be angry if I run
> Ahead and throw myself into his arms . . .
> Father
> I long to throw myself before anyone
> Into your arms—it's been so long a time—
> And kiss your cheek! Oh, are you angry, Mother?
> (Euripides *Iphigenia in Aulis*, 1.631-637)

It is soon revealed, despite Agamemnon's efforts at concealment, that Iphigenia is to be killed. Agamemnon cannot face his daughter or tell her the truth calmly, but it is not the daughter's feelings that concern him, it is his own.

Oh *my* fate,
August and awful! *My* misfortune.
Oh, what an evil demon is *mine*. [our italics] (1.1135).

Iphigenia bewails her coming doom at length, first pleading with her father:

But only with tears can I
make arguments and here I offer them.
O Father,
My body is a supplicant's, tight clinging
To your knees. Do not take away this life
of mine before its dying times (1, 1215–1218).

She then shows her rage over her father's abandonment of her:

He who began my life
Has betrayed me in misery
to a lonely dying. (1.1313–1315).

Finally, however, when Achilles offers to protect her, she decides to accept her death, "putting away from me whatever is weak or ignoble"(1.1377–1378) "I, savior of Greece, will win honor" (1.1383) She tells her mother not to mourn for her and not to hate Agamemnon.

It is likely that Iphigenia gives herself over to the total idealization of her father and simultaneously to the uttermost self-debasement by dying to preserve his honor. Perhaps taking her fate "like a man" is also an effort to win his approval. Agamemnon has made use of his daughter both to aggrandize himself and to debase his wife.

The husband in the Greek family is thus portrayed in constant conflict with his wife and using the daughters to hurt her. He may do this by seducing the daughters to abandon the mother. Yet, as the account of Agamemnon's behavior indicates, the daughter is not real to him as a person and he will easily abandon, expose, or even sacrifice her if he stands to achieve personal gain by such action, perhaps to buttress his own shaky ego in relationship to his wife.

Jephthah and His Daughter, Amram and Miriam, and the Hebrew Father-Daughter Relationship

Such an attitude as that described above—a husband seducing his daughter to abandon her mother and then sacrificing her—is quite unthinkable within a Hebrew covenantal family. The daughter is freed from shame of menstruation through ritual purity and does not idealize her father in the same desperate way. The father in turn does see the daughter as a real person and does not employ her against the mother.

Consider first the single example of father-daughter sacrifice in the Hebrew Bible—that of Jephthah and his daughter. As can be seen, Jephthah's path to acceptance is not an easy one (Judg. 11).

Chased away by his brothers from a share of his father's inheritance, Jephthah fled to the land of Tob where he became head of an outlaw band. However, when the Ammonites made war on Israel, the elders of Gilead brought Jephthah back to lead them in battle. Jephthah vowed that if the Lord would grant him victory over the Ammonites, then he would sacrifice as a burnt offering whatever would first come out to meet him on his return home. However, after his victory it was his only daughter who came out first to meet him.

> And Jephthah came to Mizpeh unto his house, and, behold, his daughter came out to meet him with timbrels and with dances; and she was his only child; beside her he had neither son nor daughter.
>
> And it came to pass, when he saw her, that he rent his clothes, and said, Alas, my daughter! thou hast brought me very low, and thou art one of them that trouble me: for I have opened my mouth unto the Lord, and I cannot go back.
>
> And she said unto him, My father, if thou hast opened thy mouth unto the Lord, do to me according to that which hath proceeded out thy mouth; for as much as the Lord hath taken vengeance for thee of thine enemies, even of the children of Ammon.
>
> And she said unto her father, Let this thing be done for me: let me alone two months, that I may go up and down upon the mountains, and bewail my virginity, I and my fellows.
>
> And he said, Go. And he sent her away for two months: and she went with her companions, and bewailed her virginity upon the mountains.
>
> And it came to pass at the end of two months, that she returned unto her father, who did with her according to his vow which he had vowed: and she knew no man. And it was a custom in Israel,
>
> That the daughters of Israel went yearly to lament the daughter of Jephthah the Gileadite four days in a year. (Judg. 11:34–11:40)

A striking set of genuine differences emerges between this sacrifice story and that of Agamemnon and Iphigenia. First, although both Agamemnon and Jephthah are offering a sacrifice in return for military success, Jephtha does not realize that he will be sacrificing his daughter. Rather, he offers to sacrifice "the first living creature whatsoever cometh forth of my house to meet me when I return." Second, upon seeing his daughter emerge and realizing the full import of his earlier vow, Jephthah shows genuine remorse: "He rent his clothes and said, Alas my daughter thou hast brought me very low. . . . I have opened my mouth to the Lord and I cannot go back." Thus, although his vow is ill-considered and foolish, it is not premeditated and callous in the same fashion as Agamemnon's. Furthermore, Jephthah's response to his daughter is not self-centered in the same sense as Agamemnon's is. He feels for his daughter, not only for himself. This is especially dramatic in light of the greater insecurity in Jephthah's social and political position as compared to that of Agamemnon. Nevertheless, the rabbis have been quite harsh in their evaluation of Jephthah. He is used in the Talmud as an example of one unfit to lead. They also criticize Jephthah's ignorance for not having gone to a priest or sage to have his vow annulled. (Genesis Rabbah 60:3; Midrash Tanhuma Buber Behukotai, pp. 112–114).[34]

The responses of the daughters are also quite different. Jephthah's daughter does not show the same passive idealizing response as does Iphigenia. She loves Jephthah but in a much more active way. She is willing to go along with Jephthah's vow to God because she thinks one ought not to break such vows. However, she actively goes away for two months to mourn, and the community institutes four lamentation days a year for her. There is consensus that it is wrong for a father to abandon, expose, or sacrifice a daughter.[35]

That the Hebrew father sees his daughter as a full person in her own right, one whose advice and opinions are worthy of respect and attention, finds even fuller expression in the relationship of Amram and Miriam. Miriam was the daughter of Amram and Jochebed and elder sister of Moses and Aaron. The Talmud (*Sotah* 12b), filling out the rather cryptic account in Exodus 1–2, tells that when Pharaoh decreed that all Jewish infant boys be murdered, Amram and Jochebed separated in despair over the doom impending on any children they would bear. Miriam, still a very little girl, went to her father, Amram, and argued that "Pharaoh's decree affected only the sons; your act affects daughters as well."

Amram accepted his daughter's advice and her sense of faith, and he and Jochebed remarried, Miriam dancing at their wedding. The role of the father is thus transformed from an abandoner of his daughter into her protector, the third stage of father-daughter relationships overcoming the Iphigenia complex in a way not available in the Greek attitude toward life. In due course this reunion produced Moses. Exodus 2 narrates the story of Moses' birth and the efforts of his family to hide him. When it is no longer safe to hide him in the house and his mother puts him in the little ark in the rushes, it is Miriam who is sent to watch over and protect him. She does not hesitate to approach the Egyptian princess with her plan for the child's care by his own natural mother.

The incident (Num. 27) of the five daughters of Zelophahad supports this picture of father-daughter relationships. Zelophahad had died, leaving five daughters but no sons. The five girls were as yet unmarried and therefore presumably rather young. They approached Moses with a claim that since there were no sons, they themselves should inherit the father's portion of the land and his name should not be removed from his family. The Talmud (*Baba Batra* 119b) says that the daughters argued their case wisely and to the point. Moses was impressed by them, and he brought their case straight to God Himself. God agreed with the girls' argument and praised them (Sifre, Num. 27:7). Rashi records the comment, "Happy is a person to whose words the Holy One gives agreement." Although there is no description of Zelophahad, his daughters were clearly independent and capable. They were also realistic about their father, neither idealizing him nor showing hostility to him (Num. 27:3).

The daughter's role in the Hebrew family is quite different from the son's; however, she is no less integral to the covenant. Menstruation does not cause the same shame and diminution in self-esteem as in the Greek society. Rather, it is transformed in Judaism into part of the woman's unique covenantal role. It is her task to observe carefully the laws of *nidah* and *mikva* that govern and sanctify her response to the bodily aspect of her role as a woman. The daughter's ambivalence toward the father in regard to fear of abandonment is again transformed by the covenant. Leaving the father's house to become a wife and mother on her own is a joyous and sacred fulfillment of her duty as an *eishat chayil* (a woman of valor). The Midrash recounts that when Rabban Gamaliel's daughter was getting married, he blessed her thus: "May you never return to my house and may the word *woe* never depart from your mouth." He then explained to her, "May you be so happy with your husband that you have no need to return to your parents' home; and may you have children and be devoted to raising them well" (Genesis Rabbah 26:4).

CHAPTER 11

A Covenantal View of Families: Overcoming the Two Poles of the Narcissistic Contract

In the two previous chapters we have attempted to compare respectively the position of the son in Greek versus Hebrew families and that of the daughter. On the son's side we contrasted Laius and Oedipus with Abraham and Isaac, and Rhea and Zeus and Medea and her sons with Rebecca and Jacob and Esau. On the daughter's side, we compared Clytemnestra and Electra with Naomi and Ruth, and Agamemnon and Iphigenia with Jephthah and his daughter and Amram and Miriam (see Table 6).

In this chapter we attempt to examine these dynamics from the point of view of individuation-attachment themes developed in chapters 5 through 8. This analysis depends heavily on the work of Slater

Table 6

Sons and Daughters in Greek and Hebrew Families

		Greek Families	Hebrew Families
Sons	Father	Laius–Oedipus	Abraham–Isaac
	Mother	Rhea–Zeus ------------------- Medea–Sons	Rebecca < Jacob / Esau
Daughters	Father	Agamemnon–Iphigenia	Jephthah–daughter ---------------------- Amram–Miriam
	Mother	Clytemnestra–Electra	Naomi – Ruth

(1968) on Greek families, of Bakan (1979) on Hebrew families and of Wellisch (1954) in his attempt to compare the two.

We begin with an examination of the position of the son in Greek versus Hebrew families; then we turn to an examination of the position of the daughter. The underlying questions here are how sons and daughters emerge from their positions in their families of origin to become husbands and wives (and fathers and mothers) in their own right and how a covenantal base provides the security necessary to allow the regression central to avoidance of narcissistic polarities.

Sons in Greek and Hebrew Families: A Distancing Analysis

Here we attempt to place the initial position of the son in the Greek family with regard to his father and mother separately (symbolized

Figure 18

Sons in Greek and Hebrew Families: A Distancing Analysis

A. Unresolved Oedipal Conflict (Greek Family)

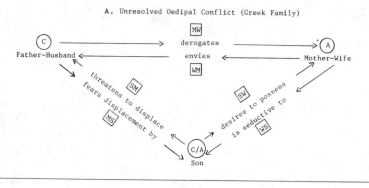

B. Ambivalently Resolved Oedipal Conflict (Greek Family)
Through Father's Evocation of Castration Threat with Regard to the Son

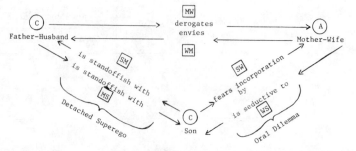

respectively by the dilemmas of Laius and Oedipus and of Rhea and Zeus and Medea and her sons) and with regard to the parental interrelationship (the Prometheus-Pandora narrative). We then analyze how this position is resolved in the Greek mind, with its attendant costs. This process is then compared to the position of the son in the Hebrew family (symbolized respectively by the stories of Abraham and Isaac and of Rebecca and Jacob and Esau and the parental story of Adam and Eve).

Figure 18a portrays the initial position of the son in the Greek family. In psychoanalytic terms the Greek husband-father is portrayed as a C position, deprecating (i.e., vagina deprecation) his wife (MW) on the one hand (and terrified of absorption by her)[36] and fearing displacement by his son (MS)[37] on the other (with his own potential threat of castration of the son). The Greek wife-mother, in contrast, is portrayed as an A position, envying (i.e., penis envy) her husband (WM) on the one hand (and terrified of abandonment by him) and attempting to seduce her son (WS) on the other. This, of course, evokes the classic Oedipal dilemma, the son wanting to displace his father (SM) and possess his mother (SW).

In distancing terms the son must be portrayed as an A/C split personality, acting in an A manner toward his A mother (wanting to

Figure 18

Sons in Greek and Hebrew Families: A Distancing Analysis (continued)

C. Unambivalently Resolved Oedipal Conflict (Hebrew Family)

Through Covenantal Circumcision

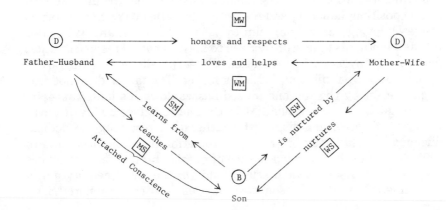

possess her) and in a C manner toward his C father (wanting to displace him). As our analysis of the Narcissus myth suggests, such an A/C split in the Greek mind is quite devastating (see the analysis of the Narcissus myth in Chapter 7). The resolution of this split can be seen as one of the benefits of the neutralization of the Oedipal dilemma. Let us suggest how this is accomplished by building on classic psychoanalytic thinking.

The father counters the son's threat of displacement by activating his own threat of castration. This serves to neutralize rather than to resolve the son's desire to displace the father, resulting in the mutual standoffishness in the father-son relations (both MS and SM=C) diagrammed in Figure 18b. The husband-wife relationship, however, remains unchanged, the husband still deprecating his wife (MW=C) and the wife sill envying her husband (WM=A). As such, the mother will still try to seduce her son (WS=A). The orientation of the son to his mother is dramatically transformed, however. The son gives up his desire to possess his mother, now fearing incorporation by her (SW=C). In other words, the neutralization of the Oedipal dilemma between son and father leads to (or at least fails to resolve) the oral-narcissistic dilemma between son and mother.

In summary, the son overcomes his initial A/C split in personality by becoming a C uniformly—with both his father and mother. This prepares him to take a C position in his own subsequent role as husband and father. As the superego is presumably internalized in this process, morality for the man must thus have an isolated, detached quality to it.

The position of the son in the Hebrew family is diametrically different (see Figure 18c). The covenantal matrix within which the son develops, symbolized by circumcision (*berith hamilah*), changes all of the familial relationships. The Hebrew husband may be diagrammed as a D position, honoring and respecting his wife (MW). She in turn is also a D, loving and helping him to pass on the covenant (WM). Her role as a mother is to nurture her son to his covenantal responsibilities, dampening any sexual provocation (WS=D). The son in turn overcomes the oedipal dilemma with his father. The father does not fear displacement by the son and indeed passes down his inheritance, instructing him in the covenant (MS=D). The son gives up his desire to possess his mother and displace his father (thus resolving the Oedipal dilemma), instead coming to accept protection from his father and to learn from him. It is this assurance of outside protection that allows the son to enter and temporarily remain in the undefined state of a discipline (SM= B). The son does not fall into the oral-narcissistic dilemma with his mother, neither fearing incorporation by her nor desiring to possess her. He comes to trust her not to use him for her own interests and allows her to nurture him and comes to learn from her (SW=B).

This change of view is symbolized by covenantal circumcision but extends to the idea of covenant in general. The father knows the son will inherit the covenant and thus need not try to displace the father; the son knows the father could have castrated him but did not. The mother's change in the covenantal family is pivotal. She transforms from seductress to nurturer-mediator, dampening the Oedipal dilemma between father and son and the oral dilemma between mother and son.[38]

Parents relate in a D manner to their sons and to each other. Further, the parents provide the genuine protection and nurturance necessary to allow the son to accept the temporary and necessary non-definition of the child and student (the B position) and slowly advance on the BED axis, whereby he slowly acquires his own limits and becomes a D in his own subsequent role as a husband and father. The son's trust in his parents not to exploit his necessary dependency is essential to covenant and makes it unnecessary for the son to seek illusory safety in the mirroring narcissistic position (C). The basis for the male covenantal conscience can thus ultimately be seen to involve individuated attachment (cell D) rather than the narcissistic and removed detachment (cell C) emergent in the Greek family.

Daughters in Greek and Hebrew Families: A Distancing Analysis

Here we attempt to place the initial position of the daughter with regard to her father and mother separately (symbolized respectively by the dilemmas of Clytemnestra and Electra and of Agamemnon and Iphigenia) and to the parental interrelationship (the Prometheus-Pandora narrative), and to analyze how this position is resolved with its attendant costs. This process is then compared to the position of the daughter in the Hebrew family (symbolized respectively by the stories of Naomi and Ruth, of Jephthah and his daughter, of Amram and Miriam, and of the parental narrative of Adam and Eve).

Figure 19a portrays the initial position of the daughter in the Greek family. As before, the Greek wife-mother is portrayed as an A position, envying her husband (WM) on the one hand (and terrified of abannment by him) and afraid of abandonment by her daughter (WD) on the other (with her own potential threat of eliciting shame of menstruation in the daughter). The Greek husband-father, in contrast, is portrayed as a C position, deprecating his wife (MW) on the one hand (and terrified of absorption by her) and willing to abandon, expose, or sacrifice his daughter (MD) on the other. This, of course, evokes the classic Electra dilemma for the daughter; she willing to abandon her mother (DW) to identify with her father (DM).

In distancing terms the daughter must be portrayed as an A/C split personality, acting in an A manner toward her C father (wanting to identify with him) and in a C manner toward the A mother (wanting to abandon her). The resolution of this potentially devastating split (again see the previous analysis of the Narcissus legend in Chapter 7) can be seen as one of the benefits of the neutralization of the Electra dilemma. Let us suggest how this is accomplished by building on classic psychoanalytic thinking.

The mother counters the daughter's threat of abandonment with an activation of the daughter's shame of menstruation, thus lowering the daughter's sense of self-esteem. This serves to transform rather than to resolve the daughter's desire to abandon her mother into a symbiotic clinging with her, which is, of course, returned (both FD and DF=A) as diagrammed in Figure 19b. The wife-husband relationship, however, remains unchanged, the wife still envying her husband (WM=A) and the husband still deprecating his wife (MW=C). As such, the father will still try to abandon his daughter (MD=C). The daughter in turn still identifies with the father (DM=A). In other words, the neutralization of the Electra dilemma (between mother

Figure 19a

Daughters in Greek and Hebrew Families: A Distancing Analysis

A. Unresolved Electra Conflict (Greek Family)

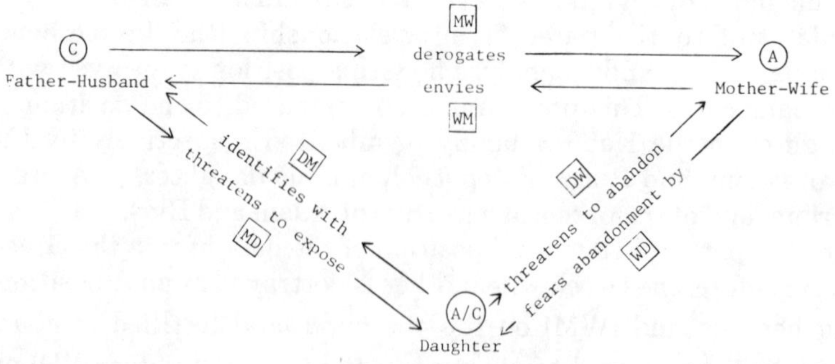

and daughter) leaves the oral-narcissistic dilemma (between father and daughter) unchanged.

In summary, the daughter overcomes her initial A/C split in personality by becoming an A uniformly—with both mother and father. This further prepares her to take an A position in her own subsequent role as wife and mother. As the ego ideal presumably is internalized in this process, morality for the woman must thus have an embedded, deindividuated quality to it.

The position of the daughter in the Hebrew family is diametrically different (see Figure 19c). The covenantal matrix within which the daughter develops is symbolized by ritual purification regarding her menstruation (*nidah* and *mikva*) and fundamentally changes all of the familial relationships. The Hebrew husband may be diagrammed as a D position, honoring and respecting his wife (MW). She in turn is also a D, loving and helping him to pass on the covenant (WM). Her role as a mother is to help guide her daughter into a similar role, accepting her femininity without shame (WD=D). The daughter then gives up any attempt to abandon her mother and ally with her father (thus resolving the Electra dilemma), instead coming to accept nurturance from her mother without being symbiotically connected to her, and to learn from her. It is this assurance of outside nurturance that allows the daughter to enter and temporarily remain in the undefined state of a student (DW=B). The daughter does not fall into the oral-narcissistic dilemma with the father, neither fearing abandonment by him nor desiring to fuse with him. She comes to trust him not to use her for his own interests, allows him to protect her, and comes to learn from him (DM=B).

Figure 19b

B. Ambivalently Resolved Electra Conflict (Greek Family) Through Mother's Elicitation of Menstrual Shame with Regard to the Daughter

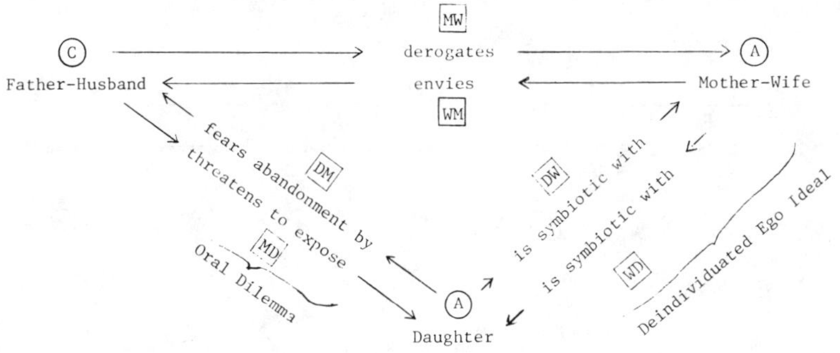

This change of view is symbolized by covenantal purification but extends to the idea of covenant in general. The mother knows the daughter is a partner to the covenant and that she need not try to abandon the mother; the daughter knows the mother will not evoke menstrual shame in her. The father's change in the covenantal family is pivotal. He is transformed from child exposer to protector, dampening the Electra dilemma between mother and daughter and the oral dilemma between father and daughter.

Parents relate in a D manner to their daughters and to each other. Further, the parents provide the genuine protection and nurturance necessary to allow the daughter to accept the temporary and necessary nondefinition of the child and student (the B position) and slowly advance on the BED axis. She acquires her own limits and becomes a D in her own subsequent role as wife and mother. It is the daughter's trust in her parents not to exploit her necesary dependence that is the essence of covenant and makes it unnecesary for the daughter to seek illusory safety in the idealizing narcissistic position (A). The basis for the female covenantal conscience can thus ultimately be seen to involve individuated attachment (cell D) rather than the narcissistic and deindividuated symbiotic connection (cell A) emergent in the Greek family.

Parent-Child Relationships: A Comparative Appraisal

Table 7 presents a comparative appraisal of the role of parent-child relationships in Greek and Hebrew families. What becomes clear is that the ambivalent resolution of same-sex parent-child conflicts in

Figure 19c

C. Unambivalently Resolved Electra Conflict (Hebrew Family)
Through Covenantal Purification

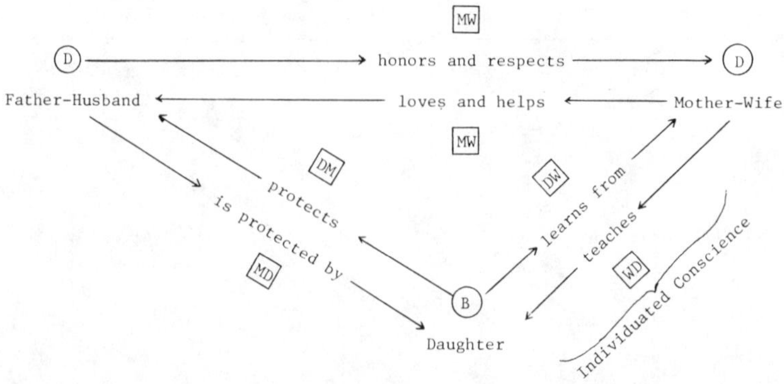

Table 7

Parent-Child Relationships in Greek and Hebrew Families

	Sons		Daughters	
	with Fathers	with Mothers	with Fathers	with Mothers
Greek Families	1. son threatens displacement of father; father fears displacement by son (Oedipal Dilemma)	1. son wants to possess mother; mother wants to seduce son	1. daughter idealizes father; father wants to abandon daughter	1. daughter threatens abandonment of mother; mother fears abandonment by daughter (Electra Dilemma)
	2a. father threatens castration of son, neutralizing son's threat of displacement	2a.	2a.	2a. mother evokes menstrual shame in daughter, neutralizing daughter's threat of abandonment
	3a. father and son standoffish with each other; introjection of detached superego (C)	3a. son fears incorporation by mother; mother wants to seduce son (Narcissistic Dilemma)	3a. daughter fears abandonment by father; father wants to abandon daughter (Narcissistic Dilemma)	3a. mother and daughter symbiotically fused with each other; introjection of deindividuated ego-ideal (A)
Hebrew Families	3b. covenantal circumcision allows son to regress to disciple role and learn from father (B)			covenantal purification allows daughter to regress to disciple role and learn from mother (B)
	3c. son becomes mature adult and introjects healthy conscience (D)			daughter becomes mature adult and introjects healthy conscience (D)

Greek families (i.e., the Oedipal conflict and the Electra conflict) creates or fails to remove the potential for violence in the cross-sex parent-child relationships (the narcissistic dilemmas of mother "seduction" or murder of son; father "exposure" or abandonment of daughter). This is exactly the finding of Philip Slater (1968) on Greek mythological families.

Aggression in cross-sex parent-child dyads in Greek families occurs in the myths more than twice as often as aggression in same-sex parent-child dyads (Slater, 1968, p. 403). Slater points out that this finding runs counter to the cornerstone of orthodox psychoanalytic thinking. The pattern becomes understandable in light of the analysis above. The ambivalent resolution of the Oedipal and Electra dilemmas available from the Greek perspective (cf. Wellisch, 1954) transfers parent-child conflicts from the same-sex arena to the cross-sex arena.

Wellisch also suggests, as do we, that the biblical perspective provides unambivalent and full resolution of the Oedipal and Electra conflicts. This should drastically reduce cross-sex parent-child conflicts. Indeed the work of David Bakan (1971, 1979) points to the involvement of fathers in biblical families, overcoming their tendency to abandon their children—especially their daughters—a practice widespread in both ancient and modern worlds. [39]

The ambivalent resolution of the A/C split for the children in Greek families (C fathers and A mothers) creates C sons and A daughters (see Table 8). [40] This is accomplished through the detached superego introjection for the male and the deindividuated ego ideal introjection for the female (Lewis, 1976) and leads to a re-creation of the collusive A-C parental dynamics in the next generation—the mirroring narcissistic male fearing intrusion, absorption, and intimacy; the idealizing narcissistic female fearing rejection, abandonment, and achievement (cf. Gilligan, 1982; Kohut, 1971; Napier, 1978; Rank, 1926; Willi, 1982). Covenantal circumcision and purification overcome the fear of castration and shame of menstruation inherent in the oedipal and Electra dilemmas, respectively, and producing children on the BED axis who escape the narcissistic polarities (A and C) as described by Kohut.

A covenantal ground can be seen as freeing children (and parents) from narcissistic polarities in a more general sense than in its particular circumcision and purification forms. Covenant assures a child that his/her father will protect him/her and that his/her mother will nurture him/her if he/she chooses to remain temporarily in or regress to a relatively undefined child-student role. The child simply may be unready to move ahead, and if he/she does so prematurely, he/she may

Table 8

Distancing Patterns for Sons and Daughters
In Greek and Hebrew Families

		Sons		Daughters	
		Fathers	Mothers	Fathers	Mothers
Initial Problem	1. Oedipal Dilemma / Electra Dilemma	C (want to displace)	A (are possessive toward)	A (idealize)	C (want to abandon)
Greek Family Resolution	2a. Fear of Castration / Shame of Menstruation	C (are standoffish with)	C (fear incorporation by)	A (fear abandonment by)	A (are symbiotic with)
Hebrew Family Resolution	2b. Covenantal Circumcision / Covenantal Purification	B (learn from)	B (are nurtured by)	B (are protected by)	B (learn from)

become trapped in a narcissistic position (in either its idealizing or mirroring form). This, of course, squares with Kohut's suggestion that idealizing and mirroring narcissistic disorders may emerge from earlier inadequacies in parental protection (idealizing parental object) and nurturance (mirroring parental object). Covenant overcomes these later narcissistic disorders because it provides a frame for the child to idealize and mirror at a stage when it is healthy and appropriate for him to do so.

To put it another way, a covenantal contract overcome the collusive narcissistic contract described by Willi. The covenant provides assurance that God will protect man by allowing him a state of safe retreat when he is too weakly defined to protect himself. For example, God provides clothes for Adam and Eve in their exile. God provides a fish to swallow Jonah and protect him from drowning when he is cast overboard; later, on the outskirts of Nineveh, God provides a gourd to shield Jonah from the sun. Likewise, parents in a covenantal family protect their children and set limits for them when they are still unable to do so for themselves (position B). They do this not to block the children, as in the typical Greek family, but to enable them to grow (through position E toward D). Crucial to this is the internalization of an inherited tradition to be passed down from one generation to the next, which dampens intergenerational conflict and gives each member of the family a constructive goal, something sadly lacking in the ancient Greek and contemporary American culture (see Lasch 1978).[41]

EPILOGUE

Remember ye the law of Moses my servant. Which I commanded unto him in Horeb for all Israel, Even statutes and ordinances. Behold, I will send you Elijah the prophet before the coming of the great and terrible day of the Lord. And he shall turn the heart of the fathers to the children, and the heart of the children to their fathers; Lest I come and smite the land with utter destruction. (Malachi 3:22–24)

Footnotes

1. Shestov was, however, not deeply knowledgeable in the rabbinic literature. His interpretations of the Hebrew Bible stem more from general Western philosophy, including his Kierkegaardian view of the *akedah* as a leap of faith.
2. Henri Bergson (1935) argues that the view of Socrates as a rational man has been highly Platonized. If Socrates had not been fundamentally a man of passionate commitment, Bergson asserts, he would not have submitted to his death at the hands of his fellow Athenians but like Aristotle would have fled into exile. Futher, Shestov's characterization of the scientist may represent a somewhat outmoded view (see Polanyi, 1962, on "personal knowledge").
3. Although the avoidance gradient always will be steeper than the approach gradient under this paradigm, it is possible that the approach gradient will be high enough or the avoidance gradient low enough that the two do not cross. Thus, the theoretical expectation and the experimental fact is that a rat that is very hungry and given a weak shock will approach all the way to the goal of food, perhaps becoming slightly more hesitant, instead of speeding up, as it nears the dangerous goal. The state of pure equilibirum occurs only within the range of relative strengths within which the two gradients cross.
4. Further, Miller has indicated in personal correspondence that attempts were made to compare appetite and hunger. Unfortunately, general food-satiation of an animal also cut off any specific appetite on its part. Miller believed that theoretically the appetite-pain paradigm should produce an approach steeper than avoidance gradient.
5. S. R. Hirsch [1976] expounds a different view in his commentary on Exodus (19:4). He argues that, in fact, Judaism is founded not on a *belief* that something had happened but on actual historical events seen by the whole nation; for example, the splitting of the Red Sea and the Sinaitic revelation.
6. This is not the position of all Christians on the creation story; however, it is a widely held view (see Lachs' discussion of Origen, Gregory of Nazianzus and Tertullian and Horowitz's discussion of Basil the Great, Gregory of Nyssa, Ambrose and Augustine and the hellenized Jew, Philo).
7. To be sure, the Freudian system does allow the possibility of increasing total available energy through the freeing up of that previously invested in defensive processes. Nevertheless, the Kohutian system does seem more explicitly committed to a noneconomic view.
8. Generally, one major current of the Greek mind finds a tension between order and chaos, between the civilized and the primitive, and between striving toward the height of reason and human dignity (like Aeschylus' Prometheus) and a pessimistic, almost fatalistic, surrender to the inexorable fact that man is irrational and life capricious. Uncertainty is pervasive (see Herodotus' narrative of the meeting of Solon and Croesus).
9. The increasing incidence of homosexuality among "enlightened" Jew and non-Jews may well attest to the pervasive Hellenism in modern Western society.
10. Modern biblical scholarship has erroneously accepted as axiomatic the notion that the Old Testament family must be viewed as a patriarchy (i.e., the wife, children, and household subordinate to the dominant father). Scholars steeped in a Hellenic weltanschauung ascribe to the father various degrees of power over his household—in some theories even the right to carry out capital punishment—comparable to the *patria potestas* of the early Roman Republic but not to anything in the Hebrew Bible.
11. In contrast consider the Jewish view of the woman in war. The Mishna states the everyone must join in an obligatory war, even women (Talmud, *Sotah* 44b). Jael and Judith provide well-known examples of women performing military deeds. The story of Deborah further points up the difference between Greek and Hebrew views of war and of women. Deborah accompanies the army to battle on Mount Tabor against the Canaanites. Yet she is not an Amazon. She prides herself on being a "mother in Israel" (Judg. 5:7).
    Jael who assassinated Sisera, the Canaanite general, also does not forfeit her womanhood. She is still "blessed among women in the tents" (Judg. 5:24). The contrast in views is brought to a climax in Deborah's depiction of the mother of Sisera

anticipating her son's return from the war. Surely, say her attendants, he will return soon with great booty and with women. The contrast in the treatment of female prisoners is also striking: In the Homeric epics they are fit only for rape and slavery. Indeed, the central conflict of the Iliad is woven around the quarrel between Agamemnon and Achilles over possession of a female captive. In contrast, Jewish law forbids the rape of captives and sets forth an elaborate series of regulations governing their treatment (Deut. 21:10-17 and glossators). Of course, there were instances where the Lord would require the annihilation of an entire nation as a punitive measure (e.g. Num. 31: 13-18, Deut. 25:19). Nevertheless, the aim of these commands was the punishment and destruction of evil peoples rather than the degradation of women.

12. Gordon, among others, has pointed out the very early relations between the Aegean world and the lands of the eastern Mediterranean littoral.

13. The feminist claim that in Judaism men serve only themselves by their religious scholarship whereas women must serve others is totally unfounded. The Talmud holds that study is exemplary only when the learning is used for the service of others (i.e., a Torah of *hesed*). For a self-aggrandizing use of learning (i.e., a Torah not of *hesed*), the Talmud has only scorn (see Meiselman, 1978, p. 24).

14. Although no version of the Narcissus story was, to our knowledge, ever performed on the ancient Attic stage, Euripides' *Alcestis* portrays an almost ultimate narcissistic figure. King Admetus of Pherae has learned that he is going to die unless someone is willing to die in his place. His wife Alcestis agrees. Admetus had tried to persuade his parents to die for him but they had refused. Admetus' father's response is equally narcissistic, "I gave you life, and made you master of my home and saved you. I am not obliged to die for you. I do not acknowledge any tradition among us that fathers should die for their sons. That is not Greek." (1.481-484).

15. The Midrash (Yalkut Shimoni 551) adds another scene as sequel to the biblical account. Jonah realizes that God has pardoned the people of Nineveh. He admits his error in fleeing God's command, and he now realizes the magnitude of both God's power and His mercy on His creatures. Falling on his face, Jonah says to God, "Conduct your world in your attribute of mercy" (see Bachrach, 1967, p. 70).

16. It is interesting in this context to compare the parenting of Narcissus and Jonah. The mother of Narcissus, the nymph Leirope, was raped (or at least casually impregnated) by the river-god Cephisus. The resultant intrusive-mother/absent-father pairing generally tends to produce a high incidence of schizophrenic offspring (cf. Check 1965; Reichard and Tillman, 1950; Summers and Walsh, 1979).

17. An interesting reversal in the direction of the rejection-intrusion pattern may occur at a later stage. Initially, the A person wants closeness in the attentive omnipotent other; the C person wants distance in the search for the grandiose self. Having attained this position, however, the A person may then avoid intimacy for the sake of preserving his "idealization." The C person, in contrast, may now want closeness to show off his achievement to his admiring "mirroring" other.

18. It is important to note that we use the word "regression" in a different sense than does Willi (1982). Willi basically employs the term to indicate what we label as lateral narcissistic moves from C to A (p. 76). We mean it to indicate covenantal moves from A or C back to B.

19. It is clear that Prometheus does not descend to Zeus's level of villainy, and that despite suffering he holds fast to his standard of morality and of right and wrong. His reaction may be the best possible in the face of a narcissistic Zeus, but moral autonomy, albeit heroic, is not totally adequate. Prometheus lacks the sense of trust and of the ultimate value of life that are inherent in the covenantal relationship. Unfortunately, there is no safe space for Prometheus in Zeus's world, and he is therefore isolated on a cliff at the earth's farthest edge.

20. Curiously, the modern stereotype of the devouring "Jewish mother" fits Pandora rather than Eve and is certainly descriptive of Hera as described by Philip Slater (1968). How the modern Jewish mother came to be seen in ancient Greek rather than Hebrew patterns may represent an example of the "displacement" motif whereby Western civilization attempted to artificially and incorrectly disconnect Jews and Judaism from their biblical roots.

21. See Rabbi A. I. Kook's *Musar Avicha* (pp. 34–39) for a comparable argument.
22. To a historian, Freud's reconstruction of primeval history may be ingenious and invaluable as an insight into the primal thinking of the human being; however, it can not be regarded as an actual documented historical event.
23. The possibility of the modification of instincts is accepted in many quarters of rabbinic thought, particularly the Musar teaching of Rabbi Israel Salanter and his school.
24. The mother, though seemingly the center in a sexual triangle, is again not valued in her own right.
25. A sense of participation in the covenant is experienced even among those sons for whom the law forbids circumcision for medical reasons.
26. It is noteworthy too that although the larger portion of the material inheritance generally goes to the first-born son, there is no comparable notion in carrying on the covenant. In this, all sons are equally responsible, and the leaders attain their status by means of ability and merit. Abraham, Isaac, Jacob, and Joseph were not first-born to their fathers. Neither were Levi and Judah, upon whom priesthood and kingship later devolved.
27. Covenantal circumcision must be distinguished from circumcision simply used as a rite of passage into manhood. Despite these "social benefit" arguments, Judaism stresses that only God knows the deepest reasons for the laws of Torah.
28. Wellisch (1954) employs the term "Medea complex" in *Isaac and Oedipus*. It was coined by Stern (1948).
29. Even in instances where a mother was described as less than an exemplary character, the role of motherhood was still entitled to the highest degree of honor. Respect to parents was seen as one of the commandments most difficult to fulfill (Jerusalem Talmud, Kiddushin 1:7).
30. It must be stressed again that we deal here with certain social patterns that seem to result from the observance of the Jewish laws of ritual purification. The rabbis, of course, did not believe that the laws of the Hebrew Bible were promulgated solely for the sake of these social benefits.
31. Ego ideals emerge out of earlier anaclitic identifications of a child, primarily with the mother. As psychoanalytic thinking has developed, it has become the convention to reserve the term "superego" for the punitive basis for conscience (achieved in the boy child through resolution of the Oedipus complex) and the term ego ideal for the seemingly more benign basis for conscience (available to the girl child in the resolution of the Electra complex) (cf. H.B. Lewis, 1976).
32. In a cross-cultural study Stephens (1962) finds a relationship between indices of "castration anxiety" and the severity of menstrual taboos, and one may infer not only that menstrual taboos presuppose high castration anxiety among males but also that in a society with severe menstrual taboos, penis envy and resentment of males by females is likely to be strong (cf. Slater 1968). The disorders of anorexia nervosa and amenhorrea may represent reactions to strong menstrual shame. It is interesting to note the "wasted" states of Medea and of Echo, the ultimate idealizing narcissist, in this latter regard.
33. The mother may be seen as the person who will prepare the daughter to accept her role as a woman in her marriage. Rather than elicit menstrual shame in the daughter (and subsequent penis envy), the mother may set the stage for the daughter's subsequent use of the *mikva* upon her marriage. The daughter must purify herself with regard to sexual relations with her husband but in a manner that enhances her esteem as a woman rather than diminishes it.
34. It is instructive to compare Jepthah's vow with Abraham's binding of Isaac. Jepthah's vow was a thoughtless unilateral act of no covenantal significance. Rabbinic literature, on the other hand, is commanded directly by God to offer up Isaac. This is not vow but an act required with the covenant.
35. It should be pointed out that there is some disagreement about the ultimate fate of both Iphigenia and Jephthah's daughter. While most accounts of the myth claim that Iphigenia was indeed sacrificed at Aulis by Agamemnon, one version maintains that she was miraculously snatched away to safety by Artemis at the last moment and subsequently became the priestess of a human sacrifice cult (see

Graves 1955, II, 73–80). Rabbinic and modern scholars have argued as to whether Jephthah's daughter was actually offered in sacrifice. Some say she was (Midrash Tanhuma Buber Behukotai, pp. 112–114) but others maintain that she was not put to death but instead became a recluse (see Tanach Mikraot Gedolot, glossators on Judg. 2).

36. Bettleheim (1955) argues that one illustration on this male fear of absorption by the female is the theme of "vagina dentata" (castrating vagina with teeth) in Greek art.

37. In this notation the husband-father is designated by M (man) and the wife-mother by W (woman). Son is designated by S and daughter by D.

38. This may well represent a displacement of fear of castration from the father to the mother and to women in general.

     The concept of ritual purity and impurity is demythologized by the rabbis. Talmudic discussions center around practical questions: how and when people or objects become unclean. Unclean means simply unfit to be brought into contact with the Temple and its service. There is none of the occult animistic connotation associated with words like "taboo."

39. Rostovtzeff (1964) writes that child exposure was so widespread during the Hellenistic period that it contributed toward a depopulation of Greece, few families rearing more than two children (pp. 623–625, 1329, 1547). The proportion of surviving female children was far smaller than that of male children, indicating that child exposure practices were applied especially, though not exclusively, against daughters. For example, in a papyrus letter of the first century B.C.E., Hilarion, a worker in Alexandria, sends a message to his wife in Oxyrhynchus to kill their new baby should it be born a girl. In contrast, the injunction against infanticide is clear in the Hebrew Bible. "Thou shalt not do so unto the Lord thy God for every abomination to the Lord, which he hateth, have they done unto their gods, for even their sons and their daughters they [the Canaanites] have burnt in the fire to their gods" (Deut. 12:31).

     The Israelites, too, occasionally lapsed into child sacrifice under the influence of the pagan world around them (2 Kings 6:28–31). However, the Hebrew Bible equates it with the worst of all acts of idolatry. "There shalt not be found among you any one that maketh his son or daughter pass through the fire. . . . For all that do these are an abomination unto the Lord" (Deut. 13:10–12). Yechezkel Kaufmann (1972) suggests that child sacrifice cults such as the cult of Moloch were of very limited influence in Hebrew society (pp. 139, 287).

40. Both sons and daughters accomplish this resolution through changing attitudes toward their mother, sons becoming a C with regard to her and daughters becoming an A.

41. To be sure, the structure of the covenantal family embraces its own potential pitfalls and possibilities for distortion. The danger exists that parents may pressure children excessively to follow in their footsteps (substituting their own image for the image of God). Also, biblical themes, such as sibling rivalry and birth order, may represent aberrations in the covenantal family. Riemer and Stampfer (1983) seem to see a positive expression, both historical and contemporary, of the covenantal conception in the custom of *ethical wills* (to be found in the Jewish, Christian and Muslim traditions). In this custom, parents sum up in a letter to their children their own lives and what they want most for and from these children (see Abrahams, 1926).

INDEX

Bibliography

Abravanel, I. [15th cent.] 1964. *Perush al hatorah.* 3 vols. Jerusalem: Bnai Arbael Press.
Abrahams, I. 1926 *Hebrew Ethical Wills.* 2 vols Philadelphia. Jewish Publication Society.
Aiello, J. 1972. A test of equilibrium theory: visual interaction in relation to orientation and sex of interactants. *Psychonomic Science 27:* 335-336.
Allport, G. 1937. *Personality: A psychological interpretation.* New York: Holt.
Appolodorus. *The library.* 1976. Trans. M. Simpson. Amherst: University of Massachusetts Press.
Apollonius, 1912. *Argonautica.* Cambridge: Loeb Classical Library.
Argyle, M., and J. Dean. 1965. Eye-contact, distance and affiliation. *Sociometry 28:*289-304.
Aristophanes. 1964. *Lysistrata.* Trans. D. Parker. Ann Arbor: Univ. of Michigan Press.
Aristotle. 1955. *The ethics of Aristotle.* Ed. J. Thompson. Baltimore: Penguin.
Arnold, M. 1932. *Culture and anarchy* Ed. J. Wilson. Cambridge: Cambridge Univ. Press.
Bachrach, Y. 1967. *Yonah ben Amittai Veeliyahu.* Jerusalem.
Baeck, L. 1966. *The Pharisees and other essays.* New York: Schocken Books.
Bakan, D. 1979. *And they took themselves wives: The emergence of patriarchy in Western civilization.* New York: Harper and Row.
———, 1966. *The duality of human existence: Isolation and communion in Western man.* Boston: Beacon Press.
———, 1971. *Slaughter of the innocents.* San Francisco: Jossey-Bass, Inc.
Banks, L.R. 1975. *Five women of the Old Testament.* Garden City, NY: Doubleday and Company, Inc.
Barrett, W. 1962. *Irrational man.* Garden City, NY: Doubleday.
Becker, E. 1971. *The birth and death of meaning.* New York: The Free Press.
———, 1973. *The denial of death.* New York: The Free Press.
Bem, S.L. 1974. The measurement of psychological androgyny. *Journal of Consulting and Clinical Psychology 42:*155-162.
———, 1975. Sex role adaptability: One consequence of psychological androgyny. *Journal of Personality and Social Psychology 31:*634-643.
Bergson, H. 1935. *The two sources of morality and religion.* Trans. R. Aubra and C. Brereton. New York: Holt.
Berlin, N. 1974. *Heemak Davar.* Jerusalem: El Hamekoroth Limited.
Bettleheim, B. 1955. *Symbolic wounds.* London: Thames and Hudson.
Blumenkrantz, A. 1969. *The laws of nidah: A digest.* Far Rockaway, NY.
Boman, T. 1960. *Hebrew thought compared with Greek.* Philadelphia: The Westminster Press.
Buber, M. [1948] 1970. *I and thou.* Trans. W. Kaufmann. New York: Charles Scribner's Sons.
———. [1958] 1973. *Israel and the world.* New York: Schocken Books.
———. 1961. *Two types of faith: The inter-penetrability of Judaism and Christianity.* Trans. N. B. Goldhawk. New York: Harper.
Cambridge ancient history, 1964. Cambridge: Cambridge Univ. Press.
Check, F. 1965. The father of the schizophrenic: the function of a peripheral role. *Archives of General Psychiatry 13:*336-345.
Clore, G. 1969. *Attraction and interpersonal behavior.* Paper presented to the Southwestern Psychological Association, Austin, TX.
Caro, J. [16th century] 1977. *Shulchan Aruch.* Tel-Aviv: Talman Press.
Cohen, M. [20th century] 1978. *Meshech Hochma.* Jerusalem.
Cox, H. 1965. *The secular city.* New York: The Macmillan Company.

Cuber, J.F., and P.B. Harroff. 1965. *Sex and the significant Americans*. Baltimore: Penguin Books.

Dodds, E.R. 1967. *The Greeks and the irrational*. Boston: Beacon Press.

Dover, K. 1978. *Greek homosexuality*. Cambridge: Harvard Univ. Press.

——. 1974. *Greek popular morality*. Berkeley: Univ. of California Press.

Efros, I. 1964. *Ancient Jewish philosophy*. Detroit: Wayne State Univ. Press.

Ehrlich, H., and D. Graven. 1971. Reciprocal self-disclosure in a dyad. *Journal of Experimental Social Psychology* 7:389-400.

Elijah of Vilna [18th cent.] 1954. *Perush Hagra*. New York.

Ellis, H. 1903. *Studies in the psychology of sex*. New York: Random House.

Erikson, E. H., 1963. *Childhood and society*. New York: W. W. Norton and Co.

Euripides. 1955. *Alcestis*. Ed. and trans. R. Lattimore. Chicago: Univ. of Chicago Press.

——. 1958. *The Bacchae*. Trans. D. Grene and R. Lattimore. Chicago: Univ. of Chicago Press.

——. 1958. *Iphigenia in Aulis* Trans. C. Walker, and *Electra* Trans. E. Vermeule. New York: Modern Library.

——. 1944. *Medea*. Trans. R. Warner. London: The Bodley Head.

Feldman, L. 1982. Dysfunctional marital conflict: An integrative interpersonal-intrapsychic model. *Journal of Marital and Family Therapy*, 8:417-428.

——. 1982b. Sex roles and family dynamics. In *Normal family processes*, (Ed F. Walsh) New York: Guilford Press.

Finley, J. H. 1955. *Pindar and Aeschylus*. Cambridge: Harvard Univ. Press.

Finley, M. I. 1959. *The world of Odysseus*. New York: Meridian.

Firestone, I. J. 1977. Reconciling verbal and nonverbal models of dyadic communication. *Environmental Psychology and Nonverbal Behavior* 2:30-44.

Five books of Moses with commentary of Malbim. 1964. 6 vols. New York: Grossman.

Franck, I. 1979. Spinoza's Onslaught on Judaism. *Judaism* 28, 177-193.

Freud, S. 1924. The dissolution of the Oedipus complex. Ed. and Trans. J. Strachey. *Standard Edition 19*:173-179.

——. 1923a. The ego and the id. Ed. J. Strachey and Trans. J. Riviere. *Standard Edition 19*:12-59.

——. 1923b. The infantile genital organizations: An interpolation into the theory of sexuality. Ed. and Trans. J. Strachey. *Standard Edition 19*:141-148.

——. [1915] 1917. Mourning and melancholia. Ed. and Trans. J. Strachey. *Standard Edition 14*:243-258.

——. 1914. On narcissism: An introduction. Ed. and Trans. J. Strachey. *Standard Edition 14*:73-102.

——. 1913. Totem and taboo. Ed. and Trans. J. Strachey. *Standard Edition 13*:1-161.

Fromm, E. 1966. *You shall be as gods: A radical interprestion of the Old Testament and its tradition*. New York: Holt, Rinehart and Winston.

Gayley, C. 1893. *Classical myths*. Boston: Atheneum Press.

Gilligan, C. 1982. *In a different voice: Psychological theory and women's development*. Cambridge: Harvard Univ. Press.

——. 1977. In a different voice: Women's conception of the self and morality. *Harvard Educational Review* 47:481-518.

Ginzberg, L. 1909. *The legends of the Jews*. 7 vols. Trans. H. Szold and P. Radin. Philadelphia: The Jewish Publication Society of America.

Goldberg, G., C. Kiesler and B. Collins. 1969. Visual behavior and face-to-face distance during interaction. *Sociometry 32*:43-58.

Gordon, C. 1962. *Before the Bible*. New York: Harper and Row.

——. 1966. *Ugarit and Minoan Crete*. New York: W. W. Norton.

Gouldner, A. 1965. *Enter Plato*. New York: Basic Books.

Graves, R. 1968. *The Greek myths*. Baltimore: Penguin Books.

Graves, R. and R. Patai, 1966. *Hebrew myths*. New York: McGraw-Hill.

Group for the Advancement of Psychiatry. 1982. *The process of child therapy*. New York: Brunner/Mazel, Inc.

Gutmann, D. 1980. Psychoanalysis and aging: A developmental view. In *The Course of life: Psychoanalytic contributions toward understanding personality development. Vol. III. Adulthood and th aging process.* Ed. S. Il Greenspan and G. H. Pollock. NIMH.

Harrison, J.E. 1963. *Mythology* New York: Harcourt Brace.

Hartman, H. 1964. The development of the ego concept in Freud's work. In *Essays in ego psychology.* New York: International Universities Press.

Heath, R. 1964. *The reasonable adventurer.* Pittsburgh: Univ. of Pittsburgh Press.

Henderson, J. 1975. *The maculate muse: Obscene language in Attic comedy.* New Haven: Yale Univ. Press.

Henrichs, A. 1978. Greek maenadism from Olympias to Messalina. *Harvard Studies in Classical Philology.* 82:121-160.

Herodotus. 1920–1938. *The History of the Persian Wars,* with an English translation by A.D. Godley. London: Loeb Clasical Library (4 volumes).

Hesiod. 1914. *Hesiod, The Homeric Hymns and Homerica* with an English translation by H. E. Evelyn-White. London: Loeb Classical Library.

Himmelfarb, M. 1973. *The Jews of modernity.* New York: Basic Books.

Hirsch, S. R. [19th cent.] 1976. *The Pentateuch.* 6 vols. Trans. I. Levy. Gateshead, England: Judaica Press.

The Holy Scriptures 1917. 2 vols. Philadelphia: Jewish Publication Society.

Holzman, P., and R. Gardner, 1960. Leveling-sharpening and memory organization. *Journal of Abnormal and Social Psychology 61:* 176-180.

Homer. 1924-1925. *The Iliad,* with an English translation by A. T. Murray. New York: G. P. Putnam's Sons.

———. 1924. *The Odyssey,* with an English translation by A. T. Murray. New York: G. P. Putnam's Sons.

Hooper, F. 1967. *Greek realities.* New York: Charles Scribner's Sons.

Horney, K. 1950. *Neurosis and human growth: the struggle toward self-realization.* New York: W. W. Norton.

Horowitz, M. C. 1979. The image of God in man—is woman included? *Harvard Theological Review* 72:175-206

The Jerusalem Talmud 1968. 5 vols. New York: Otzar Hasefarim.

Jourard, S. 1971. *Self-disclosure: An experimental analysis of the transparent self.* New York: Wiley.

Jung, C. G. 1969. The structure of the psyche. In *The Collected Works of C. G. Jung.* Vol. 8, Princeton: Princeton Univ. Press.

Kallen, H. 1942. *Art and freedom.* New York: Duell, Sloan and Pearce.

Kant, I. [1797] 1959. *The foundations of the metaphysics of morals.* New York: Liberal Arts Press.

Kaplan, K. J. 1977. Structure and process in interpersonal distancing. *Environmental Psychology and Nonverbal Behavior 1:*104-121.

———. Review of *Judaism and psychoanalysis* by M. Ostow. *Journal of Psychology and Judaism* (in press).

———. *TILT: Teaching individuals to live together.* Unpublished manuscript, Wayne State University.

Kaplan, K. J., I. J. Firestone, K. W. Klein, and C. Sodikoff. 1983. Distancing in dyads: A comparison of four models. *Social Psychology Quarterly 46:*108-115.

Kaplan K. J., and P. Lifshitz. 1981. Review of *And they took themselves wives: the emergence of patriarchy in Western civilization* by D. Bakan. *Journal of Psychology and Judaism 5:*133-135.

Kaplan, K. J. and C. Marks 1982. Review of *Mind and madness in ancient Greece: the classical roots of modern psychiatry* by B. Simon. *Journal of Psychology and Judaism 7:*65-66.

Kaplan, K. J., and N. Uten. Review of *The Parnas* by S. Arietti. *Journal of Psychology and Judaism* (in press).

Kaufmann, W. 1976. *Religions in four dimensions: Existential, aesthetic, historical, comparative.* New York: Reader's Digest Press.

Kauffman, Y. 1972. *The Religion of Israel,* Trans M. Greenberg. New York: Schocken Books.

Kellner, M. 1978. *Contemporary Jewish ethics.* New York: Sanhedrin Press.

Kelman, H. C. 1962. The induction of action and attitude change. In *Personality research,* ed. S. Coopersmith. Copenhagen: Menksgaard.

Kierkegaard, S. [1849] 1954. *Fear and trembling and the sickness unto death.* Trans. W. Lownil. New York: Doubleday Anchor Books.

Kohut, H. 1971. *The analysis of the self: The psychoanalytic study of the child.* Monograph No. 4. New York: International Universities Press.

Kohut, H. 1966. Forms and transformations of narcissism. *Journal of the American Psychoanalytic Association, 14:*243-272.

Koltun, E. 1976. *The Jewish woman.* New York: Schocken Boos.

Kook, A. I. 1971. *Musar avicha.* Jerusalem: Mossad Harav Kook.

Kraemer, R. 1980. Ecstasy and possession: The attraction of women to the cult of Dionysos. *Harvard Theological Review, 73:*55-81.

Lachs, S. 1974. The Pandora-Eve motif in rabbinic literature. *Harvard Theological Review 67:*341-345.

Laing, R. D., and D. Esterson, 1970. *Sanity, madness and the family.* New York: Penguin Books.

Lamm, M. 1980. *The Jewish way in love and marriage.* New York: Harper and Row.

Lasch, C. 1978. *The culture of narcissism.* New York: W. W. Norton.

Levinger, G., and D. J. Senn. 1967. Disclosure of feelings in marriage. *Merrill-Palmer Quarterly 13:*237-249.

Levovitz, Y. 1969. *Daat hochma umussar.* New York: Privately reprinted.

Lewin, K. 1935. *A dynamic theory of personality: Selected papers.* New York: McGraw-Hill.

Lewis, C. 1972. Jonah—a parable for our time. *Judaism 21:*159-163.

Lewis H. B. 1976 *Psychic war in men and women.* New York: New York Univ. Press.

Lewisohn, L. 1929. *Midchannel: An American chronicle.* New York: Harper & Brothers Press.

Locke, J. [1698] 1907. *Second treatise of government.* New York: Hafner Publishing Company.

Maertens, T. 1969. *The advancing dignity of women in the Bible.* DePere, WI: St. Norbert Abbey Press.

Mahler, M. 1968. *On human symbiosis and the vicissitudes of individuation.* New York: International Universities Press.

Maimonides, M. [12th cent.] 1962. *Mishnah Torah* 6 vols. New York: M. P. Press.

Malbim, M. [19th cent.] 1956. *Gei Hizayon.* Jerusalem: Pardes Publishing House.

Mann, T. 1927. Trans. H. T. Lowe-Porter. *The magic mountain.* New York: Alfred A. Knopf.

Marks, M. C. 1978. Heterosexual coital position as a reflection of ancient and modern cultural attitudes. Unpublished doctoral dissertation, State University of New York at Buffalo.

McAdoo, K. 1963. Speech volumes on Bell System message circuits—1960 survey. *Bell System Technical Journal* (September) 1999-2012.

Mehrabian, A., and S. Diamond. 1971. Effects of furniture arrangement, props, and personality on social interaction. *Journal of Personality and Social Psychology 20:*18-30.

Meiselman, M. 1978. *Jewish women in Jewish law.* New York: Ktav Publishing House.

The Midrash. 1961. 10 vols. Eds. H. Freedman and M. Simon. London: Soncino Press.

Midrash Samuel. 1893. Cracow.

Midrash Tanhuma [n.d.] Ed. S. Buber. Levov.

Mikraot Gedolot. 1951. 10 vols. New York: Pardes Publishing House.

Miller, N.E. 1944. Experimental studies in conflict. In *Personality and the behavior disorders.* Ed. J. McV. Hunt Vol. 1. New York: Roland.

———. 1959. Liberalization of basic S-R concepts: Extension of conflict behavior motivation, and social learning. In *Psychology: A study of a science.* Ed. S. Koch. Vol. 2. New York; McGraw-Hill.

The Minor Tractates of the Talmud. 1965. 2 vols. Ed. A. Cohen. London: Soncino Press.

Minuchin, S. 1974. *Families and family therapy.* Cambridge: Harvard Univ. Press.

Murray, G. 1951. *Five stages of Greek religion.* 3rd Edition. New York: Beacon.

Napier, A. Y. 1978. The rejection-intrusion pattern: a central family dynamic. *Journal of Marriage and Family Counselling 4:*5-12.

Niebuhr, R. 1957. The two sources of Western culture. In *The Christian idea of education.* Ed E. Fuller. New Haven: Yale Univ. Press.

Nietzsche, F. 1956. *The birth of tragedy and the genealogy of morals.* Garden City, NY: Anchor Press.

Nilsson, M.P. 1940. *Greek popular religion.* New York: Columbia Univ. Press.

Ostow, M. 1982. *Judaism and Psychoanalysis.* New York: Ktav Publishing House.

Ovid. 1955. *The metamorphoses.* Trans. M. Innes. London: Penguin Classics.

Patterson, M., S. Mullins and J. Romano. 1971. Compensatory reactions to spatial intrusion. *Sociometry 34:*114-121.

Pausanius. 1935. *Description of Greece.* 5 Vol. with an English trans. by W. H. S. Jones. Cambridge: Loeb Classical Library.

Plaskow, J. 1980. Blaming Jews for the birth of patriarchy. *Lilith 7:*11-12.

Plato. 1976. *Protagoras,* Trans. C. Taylor. Oxford: Clarendon Press.

1929. *Symposium,* with an English trans. by H. N. Fowler, W.R.M. Lamb. Cambridge: Loeb Classical Library.

———. 1926. *Timaeus.* Trans. R. G. Bury. Loeb Classical Library.

Plutarch. 1929. *Lives.* London: Loeb Classical Library.

Polanyi, M. 1962. *Personal knowledge.* Chicago: Univ. of Chicago Press.

Pomeroy, S. 1975. *Goddesses, whores, wives and slaves: Women in classical antiquity.* New York: Schocken Press.

Rank, O. [1932] 1968. *Art and artist: Creative urge and personality development.* Trans. C. F. Atkinson. New York: Alfred A. Knopf.

———. 1971. *The double.* Ed and Trans. H. Tucker. New York: New American Library.

———. 1929. *The trauma of birth.* London: Kegan Paul, Trench, Trubner.

———. 1936. *Will therapy.* New York: Alfred A. Knopf. Trans. J. Taft.

Rawls, J. 1971. *A theory of justice.* Cambridge: The Belknap Press of the Harvard Univ. Press.

Reichard, S., and C. Tillman. 1950. Patterns of parent-child relationships in mothers of schizophrenic male patients. *Psychiatry 13:*247-257.

Reik, T. 1961. *The temptation.* New York: George Braziller Inc.

Riemer, J, and Stampfer, N. 1983. *Ethical wills: A modern Jewish treasury.* New York: Schocken Books.

Rohde, E. 1925. *Psyche.* Trans. W. B. Hillis. New York: Harcourt, Brace and Company, Inc.

Rosenbloom, N. 1965. *Luzzatto's ethico-psychological interpretation of Judaism.* New York: Yeshiva University Press.

Rosenheim, E. 1980. Sexuality in Judaism. *Journal of Psychology and Judaism 4:*249-260.

Rosenstock-Huessy, E. 1969. *Judaism despite Christianity: The letters on Christianity and Judaism between (Eugen) Rosenstock-Huessy and Franz Rosenzweig.* New York: Schocken Books.

Rosenzweig, F. [1930] 1971. *The star of redemption.* Trans. W. Hallo. New York: Holt, Rinehart and Winston.

Rostovtzeff, M. 1964. *Social and economic history of the Hellenistic world.* Oxford: Clarendon Press.

Rousseau, J.J. [1762] 1912. *The social contract.* London: Allen and Company.

Samuel, M. 1950. *The gentleman and the Jew.* New York: Alfred A. Knopf.